Qu   ın Crisp was born in Sutton, Surrey, in 1908.
Aft   ty years of almost unalleviated obscurity he became
an i   nt international celebrity when a groundbreaking
TV   atization of his autobiography, *The Naked Civil*
         was shown to great acclaim in the 1970s. Crisp
      te numerous books and articles about his life and
      ions on style, fashion, and the movies. In 1981,
      oved to New York, where he wrote a variety of
      eviews and appeared in several movies (most notably
      Elizabeth I in Sally Ann Potter's *Orlando*). He died
      November 1999.

      www.AuthorTracker.co.uk for exclusive information
      on your favourite HarperCollins authors.

QUENTIN CRISP

The Naked Civil Servant

HARPER PERENNIAL
London, New York, Toronto and Sydney

Harper Perennial
An imprint of HarperCollins*Publishers*
77–85 Fulham Palace Road
Hammersmith
London W6 8JB

www.harperperennial.co.uk

This *Stranger Than* . . . edition published by Harper Perennial 2007
1

Published by Flamingo in 1985
First published in paperback by Fontana in 1977
First published in Great Britain by Jonathan Cape in 1968

A catalogue record for this book is
available from the British Library

ISBN-13 978-0-00-724168-2
ISBN-10 0-00-724168-2

Set in Galliard

Printed and bound in Great Britain by Clays Ltd, St Ives plc

Chapter One

❧

From the dawn of my history I was so disfigured by the characteristics of a certain kind of homosexual person that, when I grew up, I realized that I could not ignore my predicament. The way in which I chose to deal with it would now be called existentialist. Perhaps Jean-Paul Sartre would be kind enough to say that I exercised the last vestiges of my free will by swimming with the tide – but faster. In the time of which I am writing I was merely thought of as brazening it out.

I became not merely a self-confessed homosexual but a self-evident one. That is to say I put my case not only before the people who knew me but also before strangers. This was not difficult to do. I wore make-up at a time when even on women eye-shadow was sinful. Many a young girl in those days had to leave home and go on the streets simply in order to wear nail varnish.

As soon as I put my uniform on, the rest of my life solidified round me like a plaster cast. From that moment on, my friends were anyone who could put up with the disgrace; my occupation, any job from which I was not given the sack; my playground, any café or restaurant from which I was not barred or any street corner from which the police did not move me on. An additional restricting circumstance was that the year in which I first pointed my toes towards the outer world was 1931. The tidal wave, started by the fall of Wall Street, had by this time reached London. The sky was dark with millionaires throwing themselves out of windows.

So black was the way ahead that my progress consisted of long periods of inert despondency punctuated by spasmodic lurches forward towards any small chink of light that I thought I saw. In major issues I never had any choice and therefore the word 'regret' had in my life no application.

As the years went by, it did not get lighter but I became accustomed to the dark. Consequently I was able to move with a little more of that freedom which T. S. Eliot says is a different kind of pain from prison. These crippling disadvantages gave my life an interest that it would otherwise never have had. To survive at all was an adventure; to reach old age was a miracle. In one respect it was a blessing. In an expanding universe, time is on the side of the outcast. Those who once inhabited the suburbs of human contempt find that without changing their address they eventually live in the metropolis. In my case this took a very long time.

In the year 1908 one of the largest meteorites the world has ever known was hurled at the earth. It missed its mark. It hit Siberia. I was born in Sutton, in Surrey.

As soon as I stepped out of my mother's womb on to dry land, I realized that I had made a mistake – that I shouldn't have come, but the trouble with children is that they are not returnable. I felt that the invitation had really been intended for someone else. In this I was wrong. There had been no invitation at all either for me or for the brother born thirteen months earlier.

A brother and sister seven and eight years older than I were presumably expected though hardly, I imagine, welcome. Before any of us were born there were bailiffs in my parents' house in Carshalton.

When they moved to Sutton we by no means lived in poverty. We lived in debt. It looks better and keeping up with the Joneses was a full-time job with my mother and father. It was not until many years later when I lived alone that I realized how much cheaper it was to drag the Joneses down to my level.

As soon as I was a few days old I caught pneumonia. I was literally as well as metaphorically wrapped in cotton wool. From this ambience I still keenly feel my exile. When I was well again, I saw that my mother intended to reapportion her love and divide it equally among her four children. I flew into an ungovernable rage from which I have never fully recovered. A fair share of anything is starvation diet to an egomaniac. For the next twelve years I cried or was sick or had what my governesses politely called an 'accident' – that is to say I wet myself or worse. After that time I had to think of some other way of drawing attention to myself, because I was sent to a prep school where such practices might not have seemed endearing.

In infancy I was seldom able to vary the means by which I kept a stranglehold on my mother's attention, but on one occasion I managed to have myself 'kidnapped'. Everybody in the family always used this word to describe the incident but there were no ransom notes. I did not at that time sit on the knees of golden-hearted gangsters while they played poker in rooms with the windows boarded up. The whole drama was in one act.

Our nurse told my brother and me that we were about to be taken for a lovely walk. I began as usual to deploy delaying tactics such as keeping my arms as rigid as a semaphore signaller's while she tried to put my coat on. Then as now I didn't hold with the outer world. Tired of these antics, nurse took my brother downstairs and they hid. Not knowing that they were doing this, my mother, when I asked her where they were, told me I might go just as far as the front gate to look for them. I went not only to the gate but out into the street and down to the corner of the Brighton Road. There I met a rag-and-bone man who offered me a lift in his hand-cart.

I was found on Sutton Downs two or three miles from home by one of my mother's friends. Only about two hours had passed, but the whole neighbourhood had been stirred up and my mother had telephoned the police. This was nice. Unfortunately the doctor who examined me on my return advised my mother never to question me about the incident. That was a pity, for now I can remember nothing of my journey.

For many years I was troubled by two half-formed memories. In one the ground is covered with crumpled newspapers. I put my hands on these and move them about but I never lift any of them up. Underneath is something unpleasant. To this day I have no idea whether this has something to do with my ride in the hand-cart or not. Perhaps one should regard the kidnapping as just the first instance of my being picked up by a strange man at a street corner.

The other memory was of drawing something long – a thin tube, a piece of cord – between my finger and thumb. I felt that there were lumps inside the tube. The sensation was faintly nasty. One day when I was at least forty I was lying in bed having another go at my half-buried past when I saw in detail the coverlet that had been on my cot when I was a baby. This had ribs of twisted white wool running across it, and round the edge was a lace border with small loops in it that I felt if I pulled the coverlet up to my chin. At the same time that I saw these details, I remembered that in this cot I slept beside my parents' bed. One night I heard my parents whispering. Then my mother called

8

my name tentatively – experimentally. I knew that on no account must I answer. The whispering began again and, after a while, my father gave a long, despairing groan. I was surprised at this because I had expected, not him, but my mother to be hurt. It is a pity that I cannot say that, when I recalled all this, the scales fell from my eyes and the meaning of my life was suddenly clear. I merely experienced a pleasant relief as though I had solved a clue in a long-abandoned crossword puzzle. The only practical use I ever found for this revelation was that it enabled me to answer with certainty one of the questions that doctors and psychologists always asked me. Did my parents ever make love after I was born? I never know how they imagined I would be able to answer but I could.

Sad to say the greatest scandal in Sutton during my childhood came and went without my being able to convert it to my own use, though I perched on the knee of its central character. Moreover, while I sat thus, he powdered my face and declared openly that I was his favourite. A production of *A Midsummer Night's Dream* was being put on at the preparatory school to which my two brothers went. To give it a professional gloss, a down-and-out actor, who showed us photographs of himself wearing nothing but a bunch of grapes, had been engaged as director.

It is an instance of my mother's spasmodic indulgence of me that I was allowed to appear in public wearing a wreath of roses and a green tulle dress in a show that was in no other way transvestite. The play was not being acted solely by the boys of the school. My sister had a walk-on part and a Miss Benmore, draped in mauve chiffon, sat in the middle of the stage on a seat that at home was called the 'rug box' and usually stood in our hall. I danced myself silly but only when I fought with another fairy for a place that I felt was really mine did

9

the applause become as loud and as sincere as I felt it should be.

The London actor had evidently played Bottom in more senses than one for next day he was seen by my sister on Sutton station in handcuffs. Later, the headmaster of my brothers' school telephoned my mother and begged her not to let any of us see the local papers. The actor had been charged with seducing one of the boys. I was too young to know that I had lived a little while.

While I spent all my time at home, my mother can hardly have known even a short spell when she was not worried about me. Sometimes she tried cosseting me and sometimes she tried upbraiding me while, after one of my 'accidents', she washed my stinking knickers. I wept but I never really felt guilty. I thought my vomit, my faeces, my tears were love gifts to my mother – no more disgusting, after all, than a broken heart.

My lust for praise was inordinate. Only the servants made any attempt to satisfy it. For them I danced incessantly and recited poems that I made up as I went along. I did not realize, when they applauded me, that clapping might merely be a welcome change from dusting. If my mother called me down from some upper room that the housemaid was supposed to be cleaning, I did not obey until she was really angry. Then I could cry.

My father did not like me. My presence was insistently physical. He was a fastidious man. He dusted the chair on which the cat had been lying before occupying it himself. He ate a banana with a knife and fork – to modern minds a dead give-away if ever there was one. In later years I had to supply various subsidiary kinds of fuel for the furnaces of his hatred. In infancy my existence was enough.

So my parents and I constructed between us the classic triangle for all the world as if we had read the right books on psychology, but although (or because) my mother was so close to me, she did not realize that I was gradually coming to require not love so much as unconditional obedience.

Chapter Two

❧

Even in childhood I was mad about men in uniform.

As in a silent movie, when thirty long years had passed, I went back to the place of my birth to pose in the art school there. Passing through the railway station, I saw, with that inward eye that is the curse of solitude, my sister squatting by the ticket office to play with a baby bear that a sailor held on a lead. He stood for a while watching my sister and I watched him.

I also remember the soldiers that were billeted in private houses in Sutton during the First World War. To most people they represented a domestic inconvenience bravely borne but to me they were emotionally disturbing. When they marched away to Flanders, the girls lined the streets and, with delicious sadness, threw sweets to them. It all seemed wistful and romantic at the time. I had never then heard any of the things men say about women making fools of themselves.

When the First World War was about half over and people had given up saying that it would only last a few weeks and taken to prophesying that it would go on for ever, my father suffered his first defeat in the presence of the Joneses. He moved us all into a smaller house on the opposite side of the road. The only thing that worried me here was that I lost my captive audience. There were no rooms and, presumably, no money for servants who lived in. In the modern world where servants are extinct it is difficult to realize that to my parents this change in their circumstances must have been rather like the Fall. The only thing that made the situation bearable for them was that, because it was wartime, all economies could be made to look like patriotic gestures.

We moved into this new home when I was seven and out again when I was ten and it is here that my definite childhood recollections begin. Of the two houses that I had lived in previously my memories are sharp, but have no chronology. Their background is hazy or even false but if anyone were to utter the name of our wartime house, all the quality of my life there would come back to me. This house was almost the last in the road. My memory always looks towards the empty fields and the poplar trees standing along the mauve-grey paths that zigzagged slightly uphill towards Belmont and the school to which I then went. The sky is sunless, the earth unpopulated; and, to my waking eyes, this landscape is for ever in a state of pause without the least hint of expectancy. This is also the setting for my most persistent childhood dream and in the nightmare foreboding is everywhere. I look at each poplar tree in turn until I catch a glimpse of a figure hiding behind one of them – a woman in a black hat and a grey cloak. As soon as I see her, she starts to come towards me along the path. She travels at great speed, but her cloak gives no sign that her legs are moving. I do not cry out; I do not run away. The dream has no ending.

Although I did not think about this nightmare during the day, I seldom went out of doors wantonly. If I left the house by myself it was usually to visit one or other of two girls of about my own age. I had no friends who were boys because boys wanted to fight. I knew I would get hurt and not win. Also they would not play my games of make-believe. But girls could be made to do as I said if I shouted at them or hit them or, in the last resort, deserted them. In case the desertion might come as a relief, I always remembered to cry loudly as I ran through their front gates so that someone would hear and scold them for not being a 'good little hostess'. All the games I played with these little girls were really only one game. We dressed up in their mothers' or even grandmothers' clothes, which we found in box rooms and attics, and trailed about the house and garden describing in piercing voices the splendours of the lives that in our imaginations we were leading. 'This wheelbarrow is my carriage. I gather up my train as I get in. Get in the other side, you fool. I nod to the servants as I leave. No. I ignore them. I am very proud and very beautiful.' This kind of monologue I could keep up for whole afternoons.

I cannot say whether my mother led me into this lifelong exotic swoon because it was secretly her own ideal or whether, finding me already there, she sustained me in it as a way of keeping me quiet. Undoubtedly she allowed me to feel that it was a taste we shared. The first grown-up entertainment to which she ever took me was *Chu Chin Chow*. In this play a certain Miss Brayton, wearing saucers on her breasts and a kind of dirty-clothes basket on her head, walked up and down stairs with her hands at the utmost horizontality. I nearly fainted with delight. The first paintings that I consciously looked at were Lord Leighton's classical mock-ups. My introduction to literature was of a piece with these other cultural initiations. My mother read to me from *The Lady of the Lake* and the *Idylls of the King*. She used the 'poetry' voice but she read extremely well – possibly because she was made to read the same pieces so often. When she decided that it was time for me to read to myself she handed me fairy stories and from them I graduated to the works of Mr Haggard. Having exhausted these I gave up reading altogether and from then on held a view of literature which I can best express by this anecdote.

A friend of mine had a landlady who, when she saw him putting on his hat and advancing towards the front door, would say, 'Going out.' Should she find him at the sink, holding his kettle under the running tap, she would say, 'Filling your kettle.' These and other such phrases were not questions; they were statements. Because they were made with a smile, they were meant to show that she approved and was, in a remote way, taking part in his life. One day she entered a room where he was sitting with his eyes turned towards an open novel. She said, 'Waiting.'

Once while I was engaged in sharing my gauzy internal dream with one of my little friends, a faint breath of criticism ruffled the garden where we played. A quite unnecessary cousin of my playmate was present and she suggested that, to bring a little true romance into our game, she should stand on the veranda and watch with green eyes while her lover (me) walked by with my friend on my arm, talking and laughing and paying no heed. For a moment I was absolutely disorientated. I realized an effort was being made to edge me into the disgusting role of a handsome prince. Then my hostess said, 'Oh, Denis (as my name was before I dyed it) never plays the part of a man.' I do not recall that she had any difficulty in saying this or that her cousin took more than a moment to reply, 'Oh well, I'll be the prince and he can stand on the veranda.' The moment passed and I moved back into the dream.

Occasionally I tried to drag my brother into my world of make-believe. I rarely succeeded. No wiles of mine – not even my tears (and tears were to me what glass beads were to African traders) – could buy his companionship for long. I learned very early in life that I was always going to need people more than they needed me.

To most children I suppose there is a difference in degree between their imaginary and their real lives – the one being more fluid, freer and more beautiful than the other. To me fantasy and reality were not merely different; they were opposed. In the one I was a woman, exotic, disdainful; in the other I was a boy. The chasm between the two states of being never narrowed.

At home I managed to make my life miserable more or less unaided. At school this was done for me. Teachers could not refrain from scoring off me as soon as they perceived that I had no armour. When some of the pupils had gone into Sutton to take a music examination, I happened to be the last to come back into the school. The headmistress asked me if I thought that I had passed. I replied that I did – that the exam had been quite easy. There was a roar of laughter from everyone. Only then did I realize that I ought, as a formality, to have said the exam was difficult.

Finding myself the constant object of amused attention was hateful to me yet I don't remember feeling the slightest embarrassment at arriving from time to time at school with my upper half awash with tears and my lower half dripping with excrement.

At my preparatory school I won a very poor scholarship to a public school on the borders of Staffordshire and Derbyshire. Before I went there, during a routine fit of weeping, my mother warned me that I would not be able to go on like that at boarding school. I never did. I was half-starved, half-frozen and humiliated in a number of ways, but I never felt the faintest desire to cry. Fear and hatred do not seem to find expression in tears.

This school was on the top of a hill so that God could

see everything that went on. It looked like a cross between a prison and a church and it was.

For about a year I was preoccupied only with survival – learning the rules, lying low under fire and laying the blame on others. When at length these things became second nature to me, I had a timorous look round and saw that the whole school was in an even greater ferment of emotion than my prep school had been, but here the charge ran from the older to the younger boys rather than between the staff and the pupils.

For details of the love life of the prefects, which was one of our abiding preoccupations, you could ask one of the boys whose vocation was to carry notes from the prefects to the ordinary boys. (They were forbidden to speak to one another.) I was once in a class when the master said to one of these procurers, 'What's that?' A piece of paper was handed over my head from the boy to the master. When he saw it, he said, 'What are these names? Why are they bracketed together?' 'They're just names,' said the boy and this he repeated to all the questions that were fired at him. Finally the paper was handed back and the class continued. At length, the great scandal, that we had all so longed for, occurred. It was to the school what the Mrs Simpson affair was to England.

The ground plan of the college was an 'H'. Four classrooms were on each of two opposing arms of this figure and there were two dormitories on each of the two floors above these rooms. Thus there were four 'houses' on each side of the building – an irresistible Romeo and Juliet set-up.

One night, though Montague arms reached out to him from three dormitories besides his own, a boy descended two flights of stairs, traversed the crossbar of the 'H' and climbed two flights of stairs on the other wing to keep a tryst with a Capulet. Now, in the winter of my life, feeling that Shakespeare's Romeo might just as well have married the girl next door, I realize that these two schoolboys could have met behind some dreary haystack almost any afternoon. What the older boy did, he did not for love alone, but in order to defy the authorities with all the world on his side. He was caught. By lunchtime the next day the whole school knew every detail of this mad escapade.

His sin was the occasion of the only public beating that I have ever witnessed. The entire school was assembled in the big hall and seated on benches on either side of the room. In the open space in the middle the modern Romeo bent over and the headmaster ran down the room to administer the blows. After the first two strokes the younger brother of the victim left the room. Even now I can't help wishing that we had all done the same. What made this exhibition so disgusting was not the pain inflicted. Today a go-ahead schoolmaster would say, 'This delights me more than it delights you.' In many parts of London, such goings-on are just another way of making a party go with a swing. What was almost insufferable was that a simple form of self-gratification should be put forward as a moral duty. Before that day I had disliked the head; afterwards I hated him.

I think that all the boys felt a little shaken, frightened, degraded. At least no one seemed to regard what they had seen as right. Some of us enshrined the culprit in our hearts as one of the saints of Aphrodite. He was, of course, expelled at once to prevent a snowstorm of 'fan' notes but he had the nerve to turn up again at a later date. I don't think that I ever spoke a word to him, but now, when I saw him throwing a cricket ball about with some other boys (well out of sight of any member of the staff), I watched him greedily. He was a thick-set young man with black hair growing low on his forehead. His expression was brutish and mocking – very desirable.

Unlike our Miss Capulet I myself never lured any of the boys to their doom. This was not for want of trying but for lack of any physical advantages. I was very plain. My rich mouse hair was straight but my teeth were not. I wore tin-rimmed spectacles. In spite of this formidable natural chastity belt, I did spend one night in bed with another boy. He was the only Indian in the school and, when his arrival in our dormitory was heralded, I hoped that he might be some unimaginable animal given to fits of terrible rage. This was not so. Sexually he was a little more precocious than the other boys and went with prostitutes during the holidays but, in all other respects, he was only as dangerous as the rest. Our sleeping together was part of the thinly spread orgy that was a ritual on the last night of every term. The occasion could only be described as a success in as much as the object of the exercise was to do it and to be known to have done it. These ends were achieved. I did not expect any pleasure and there was none. I did not even experience a sense of sin. The intimations of immorality had come and gone some time back.

As soon as I was old enough to wash myself, I had begun the habit of staying in the bath until my body passed from lobster-pink to scum-grey. While lying in one of these semi-submerged trances, in a boarding house in Queen's Gate to which my parents moved temporarily, I discovered the only fact of life that I have ever fully understood. Masturbation is not only an expression of self-regard: it is also the natural emotional outlet of those who, before anything has reared its ugly head, have already accepted as inevitable the wide gulf between their real futures and the expectations of their fantasies. The habit fitted snugly into my well-established world of make-believe.

When I awoke the morning after my first orgasm, I remembered it instantly and wondered if I should die, go mad or contract some incurable disease. After a few days it became obvious that I was to experience no noticeable physical ill-effects. Cosiness was restored. About my immortal soul I did not worry. Vice is its own reward. It is virtue which, if it is to be marketed with consumer-appeal, must carry Green Shield stamps. The greenest of these is the 'sweet bye-and-bye'. For me this stamp is not negotiable. The one thing I would not wish on my worst enemy is eternal life.

I think I can say that effeminate homosexuals are among those who indulge least in sex acts with other boys at school. They seem to realize that these jolly get-togethers are really only a pooling of the carnal feelings of two people who deep down are interested in their dreams of girls. Otherwise they tend to be self-congratulatory pyrotechnical displays of potency.

Certainly I felt this to be so. I longed to be the subject of a school-shaking romance, but relationships in which personality was not involved were valueless to me. What I wanted most of all was to use sex as a weapon to allure, subjugate and, if possible, destroy the personality of others. Holding this view I was naturally more interested in the masters than in my mere equals. I tried to seduce them all the time. I worked hard at lessons or at least hard enough to shine. Thus I forfeited all friendship with the other boys. This scarcely mattered as most of them disliked me so much already.

Worst of all from their point of view, I was openly eager to take exams. Possibly exams are more difficult now than they used to be. At my school the early ones could be passed by an effort of memory alone. I used to go into the examination room with pale lips mumbling whole vocabularies of Latin military words and come out again thoroughly relaxed, knowing nothing. Even geography could be dealt with in this way. I learned by heart the names of the towns on the L.M.S. Railway. Of course, if a dot had been missing from the map, I would have arrived in Edinburgh with a town in hand, but the examiners were seldom as unkind as that. With their generous help I got into the sixth form when I was fifteen.

Once this standard had been achieved, I felt the tide beginning to turn. I do not mean that at last the boys started to respect me but that now the masters began to hate me too. I had reached the limit of my educability. It slowly dawned on the staff that they had spread their brooding pinions over a boy who had no more than a crossword-puzzle mentality. I was the opposite of a chimpanzee. I could memorize but I could not infer results from causes. Out of sheer disillusionment, the masters allowed themselves to be hoodwinked by the specialization racket. I went to the Latin master and said, 'I'm afraid I'll have to give up Latin this term, sir – dear old Latin – but I've so much geography to do.' Then I went to the geography master and said, 'I'm afraid I'll have to give up geography – dear old geography, etc.' After a lot more speeches of this kind, my time-table became an arid waste. For my final two years I sat in a Nissen hut and read trashy novels by Susan Glaspell.

I was at boarding school for four years. During that time I learned only one thing that I was ever able to use in adult life. I discovered that my great gift was for unpopularity. At first I would have done anything to shed it. I tried feverishly to develop protective colouring. Then these endeavours became fitful, alternating with essays in deliberate provocation. Finally I mastered my medium. It became an armour – almost a weapon. I had passed that barrier of which Mr O'Connor speaks in the *Memoirs of a Public Baby*. I had learned consciously to achieve an effect that originally I had produced by accident. I must have been very unpopular indeed. To this day I have a tiny mark on my wrist where boys sawed through the flesh with a jagged ruler. For this and other reasons, I hated school but it was as well that I went there. It provided a dress rehearsal for the treatment that I was to receive in the streets of London in a few years' time.

During my last term my father had written a desperate letter (doubtless dictated by my mother) to my classics master asking him what on earth was to be done with me. The reply stated that I had not the makings of a scholar. I suppose that a classical training helps one to put things mildly. It was suggested that, as I seemed to have an ability to write, I should try to enter the field of journalism. The teacher had to say something positive and, having no knowledge of anything that had happened in the world since Thermopylae, did not understand that I was totally unsuited to this profession. Above all else, a journalist must be able to get on with strangers. Nevertheless I went to London University to take a course in journalism.

I did not protest at the absurdity of this. I dared not. I had nothing to suggest in its place and I knew that, while I sat dreaming through the lectures, at least I was putting off for another two years my terrible confrontation with the outer world.

Chapter Three

❧

I was now eighteen and beginning to feel really uneasy about the future – openly on the grounds that I was so inadequate to earn a living, and secretly because I suspected that sexually I was quite unlike anyone else in the world. Friends were starting to ask me questions about my private life. Their intention was not unkind, but I was filled with misgiving.

'Are you keen on this girl you talk so much about?' a friend of my mother asked. 'Good God, no,' I replied putting on a face as though I had just stepped in something. Then I hastily embarked upon a cynical diatribe against all human sentiments. This was the kind of conversation that my mother's friend loved but I now think that I wasted a rather wonderful woman. If I could simply have told her that, to my bewilderment, I did not think that I was ever going to be able to take a sexual interest in any girl, I'm sure she would have listened. This would have been at least a thin rope flung from my tiny island towards the mainland.

She would not have believed me, because in those far-off days a homosexual person was never anyone that you actually knew and seldom anyone that you had met. She would have thought that I had chosen at random a peculiarity that would make me more interesting but she would not have been shocked. She was my first glimpse of the *vie de bohème*.

Her name was Mrs Longhurst, a big striding strident person of about forty ('I'm longing for one of those bonnets with jet beads on them'). By profession she was a stewardess and sometimes a portrait model ('Who cares as long as it brings in some money?'). She lived in Charlotte Street ('I adore all foreigners') in a room whose walls were covered with African knives. Her other room she had let to a nurse who had attended my mother during her four years in various nursing homes. After a while this nurse came to dislike Mrs Longhurst, but at first she thought her a 'real character'. She introduced her as such to my mother and me. Mrs Longhurst took to me at once and allowed me to visit her constantly to play pontoon and talk about myself. Her mode of speech was the most exaggerated that I had ever heard. These are the words with which she warned my mother (who longed to leave Battersea) not to try Hampstead. 'Don't live in Hampstead. That's where the parents lived and they were crippled with rheumatism – bed-ridden. They moved and what happened? Within a week they were dancing in the streets of Maida Vale.' This woman did not fly to extremes; she lived there. I also soon became an adept at this mode of talk and, with the passing of the years, came to speak in this way unconsciously.

Mrs Longhurst's attitude to homosexuality, as to most things, was a mocking curiosity but she was never savage. The rest of the world in which I lived was still stumbling about in search of a weapon with which to exterminate this monster whose shape and size were not yet known or even guessed at. It was thought to be Greek in origin, smaller than socialism but more deadly – especially to children. At about this time *The Well of Loneliness* was banned. The widely reported court case, together with the extraordinary reputation that Tallulah Bankhead was painstakingly building up for herself as a delinquent, brought Lesbianism, if not into the light of day, at least into the twilight, but I do not remember ever hearing anyone discuss the subject except Mrs Longhurst and my mother. If one is not going to take the necessary precautions to avoid having parents, one must undertake to bring them up. This was what, very cautiously, I was beginning to do with my mother. My father remained invincibly ignorant.

When I left King's College, London (needless to say without a Diploma in Journalism), I could at first find no better occupation than sitting at home getting on my parents' nerves. I became so listless that my mother thought it only polite to regard me as ill. She sent me to her doctor. Without making even the most cursory examination of me he declared that all I needed was a lesson in life. My father was very annoyed. He realized that he would have to pay a consultation fee for these few glib words. He was lucky that psychology had not yet reached the middle classes. He might have had to pay much more for less. At the time, my own reaction to the doctor's remark was blank incomprehension. Later when, to vary the monotony of my existence, I took to wandering about the streets of the West End, I stumbled on the very truth that was just what the doctor had ordered. I learned that I was not alone.

As I wandered along Piccadilly or Shaftesbury Avenue, I passed young men standing at the street corners who said, 'Isn't it terrible tonight, dear? No men about. The Dilly's not what it used to be.' Though the Indian boy at school had once amazed us all with the information that in Birmingham there were male prostitutes, I had never believed that I would actually see one. Here they were for all the world to recognize – or almost all the world. A passer-by would have to be very innocent indeed not to

25

catch the meaning of the mannequin walk and the stance in which the hip was only prevented from total dislocation by the hand placed upon it.

The whole set of stylizations that are known as 'camp' (a word that I was hearing then for the first time) was, in 1926, self-explanatory. Women moved and gesticulated in this way. Homosexuals wished for obvious reasons to copy them. The strange thing about 'camp' is that it has become fossilized. The mannerisms have never changed. If I were now to see a woman sitting with her knees clamped together, one hand on her hip and the other lightly touching her back hair, I should think, 'Either she scored her last social triumph in 1926 or it is a man in drag.'

Perhaps 'camp' is set in the 'twenties because after that differences between the sexes – especially visible differences – began to fade. This, of course, has never mattered to women in the least. They know they are women. To homosexuals, who must, with every breath they draw, with every step they take, demonstrate that they are feminine, it is frustrating. They look back in sorrow to that more formal era and try to re-live it.

The whole structure of society was at that time much more rigid than it has ever been since, and in two main ways. The first of these was sexual.

The short skirts, bobbed hair and flat chests that were in fashion were in fact symbols of immaturity. No one ever drew attention to this, presumably out of politeness. The word 'boyish' was used to describe the girls of that era. This epithet they accepted graciously. They knew that they looked nothing like boys. They also realized that it was meant to be a compliment. Manliness was all the rage.

The men of the 'twenties searched themselves for vestiges

of effeminacy as though for lice. They did not worry about their characters but about their hair and their clothes. Their predicament was that they must never be caught worrying about either. I once heard a slightly dandified friend of my brother say, 'People are always accusing me of taking care over my appearance.'

The sexual meaning of behaviour was only sketchily understood, but the symbolism of clothes was recognized by everyone. To wear suede shoes was to be under suspicion. Anyone who had hair rather than bristle at the back of his neck was thought to be an artist, a foreigner or worse. A friend of mine who was young in the same decade as I says that, when he was introduced to an elderly gentleman as an artist, the gentleman said, 'Oh, I know this young man is an artist. The other day I saw him in the street in a brown jacket.'

The other way in which society in the 'twenties was rigid was in its class distinctions. Doubtless to a sociologist there were many different strata merging here and there but, among the people that I was now getting to know, there were only two classes. They never mingled except in bed. There was 'them', who acted refined and spoke nice and whose people had pots of money, and there was 'us', who were the salt of the earth.

Mitford's First Law had not then been formulated. I could have put the words 'toilet', 'mirror' and 'perfume' all into one sentence. None of the boys on the game would have noticed. I would still have been 'them' because my slight cockney accent had been flattened out a little. But they forgave me for my unfair advantages because I was in the same sexual boat as they. I took to them like a duck to ducks.

Between these twin barriers of sex and class, we sat huddled together in a café called the Black Cat. (We were not putting up with any such nonsense as 'Au Chat Noir' which was written over the window.) This was in Old Compton Street. It looked like a dozen other cafés in Soho. It had a horseshoe bar of occasionally scrubbed wood, black and white check linoleum on the floor and mirrors everywhere. The deafening glass boxes in which nowadays customers sit and eat with their ankles on view to the public had not then been built. In that happier time all was squalor and a silence spangled only with the swish of knives and the tinkle of glass as the windows of the Black Cat got pushed in.

Day after uneventful day, night after loveless night, we sat in this café buying each other cups of tea, combing each other's hair and trying on each other's lipsticks. We were waited on with indulgent contempt by an elderly gentleman, who later achieved a fame that we would have then thought quite beyond him, by being involved in a murder case. Had the denizens of the Black Cat known he was such a desperate character, they would doubtless have done much more to provoke him. As it was we only bored him by making, with ladylike sips, each cup of tea last as long as a four-course meal. From time to time he threw us out. When this happened we waltzed round the neighbouring streets in search of love or money or both. If we didn't find either, we returned to the café and put on more lipstick. It never occurred to any of us to try to be more loveable. Even if it had, I do not think we would have adopted a measure so extreme. Occasionally, while we chattered on the street corner one of our friends would go whizzing past crying, 'They're coming.' At this we would scatter. It meant that, while being questioned, one of the boys had bolted and his inquisitors were after him. At such times, if a detective saw his quarry escaping, he would seize upon the nearest prey, however innocently that person might be behaving. We treated the police as it is said you should treat wild animals. As we passed them, we never ran but, if they were already running, we spread out so that only one of our number would die. Policemen in uniform were not classed as man-eaters. I had no idea what the rules were but they never seemed to give chase; they only moved us on.

The perpetual danger in which we lived bound us together. In the café there was a lot of stylized cattiness, but this was never unkindly meant. Nothing at all was meant by it. It was a formal game of innuendoes about other people being older than they said, about their teeth being false and their hair being a wig. Such conversation was thought to be smart and so very feminine. It was better, I need hardly say, to seem like a truly appalling woman than not like a woman at all. Unfortunately in this game there seemed to be very few cards in the pack, and a whole evening spent playing it became monotonous. When we were not thus engaged, we talked about our sufferings and this I greatly preferred. Soon I had learned by heart almost every argument that could be reared in the climate of that time against the persecution of homosexuals. We weren't doing any harm; we couldn't help it; and, though this was hardly water-tight from a legal point of view, we had enough to bear already. Some speakers even went so far as not merely to excuse our sin but to glorify it, making it a source of national culture. The great names of history from Shakespeare onward were fingered over and over like beads on a rosary. We did not see that it might particularly be the offence of soliciting that was being condemned. It is hardly a matter for amazement that we did not understand this. Confusion on this point was everywhere.

The attitude of the law was arbitrary – bordering on slapdash. Boys arrested for soliciting were found guilty before they had spoken. If they did get a chance to say anything, the sound of their voices only caused the presiding magistrate to increase their sentences. I think the boys were right in assuming that they were being condemned for effeminacy. They also put forward the argument that they went on the streets because they were poor and that they were poor because they were sacked from jobs if their employers discovered them to be queer. Undoubtedly this was partly true but not entirely so. Many of the boys from the Black Cat had other jobs by day – truly improbable ones in some cases. One frail little thing was a plumber's mate. About this there were many arch jokes and much rolling of blue-lidded eyes. Young men like this one were prostitutes by vocation – blessed in infancy with gifts for serving the community in a special way.

I have known female whores who spoke very bitterly of their calling. 'If they don't like my face, they can put a cushion over it. I know it's not *that* they're interested in.' But to the boys this profession never seemed shameful. It was their daytime occupations for which they felt they needed to apologize. In some instances, these were lower class or humdrum or, worst of all, unfeminine. At least whoring was never that.

The average woman, unless she is particularly ill-favoured, regards loving and being loved as a normal part of life. If a man says he loves her she believes him. Indeed some women are convinced they are adored by men who can be seen by all to be running in the opposite direction. For homosexuals this is not so. Love and admiration have to be won against heavy odds. Any declaration of affection requires proof. So many approaches made to them are insincere – even hostile. What better proof of love can there be than money? A ten-shilling note shows incontrovertibly just how mad about you a man is. Even in the minds of some women a confusion exists between love and money if the quantity is large enough. They evade the charge of mercenariness by using the cash they extort from one man to deal a bludgeoning blow of humiliation upon another. Some homosexuals attempt this gambit, but it is risky. The giving of money is a masculine act and blurs the internal image.

I have always held the view that the union of two hearts whose incomes are equal is a complete waste of time. If anyone offered me money in exchange for sex I accepted it gladly, and by money I mean 7s. 6d. I still lived at home where 2s. 6d. a week was all the pocket money that I received. Early in life I learned that I was not going to be able to afford to set a value on myself. In consequence I have never had the bother of taking offence but can decide afresh each time that anything is offered to me whether I want it or not. Apart from my need for small change, there was another reason for accepting money. It absolved me from the charge of enjoying sex for its own sake. At home it had been explained to me that I must never say that I loved food – hardly that I liked it. How much greater the disapproval would have been for admitting that I liked sex I could only infer as the subject was seldom mentioned. To some people an offer of money is so insulting that they can accept a book token for ten shillings but not a ten-shilling note. I never needed to be offered a love token. The cash would do nicely. So far from feeling humiliated, I felt in some measure compensated for all the insults (which carried no fringe benefit of money) that I daily received from other directions.

I disliked the coarseness of the situations in which I found myself. Courtship consisted of walking along the street with a man who had my elbow in a merciless grip until we came to a dark doorway. Then he said, 'This'll do.' These are the only words of tenderness that were ever uttered to me.

The venality of my predicament I took calmly. Unlike Desdemona, I could perform the deed but not say the word.

Chapter Four

❧

My outlook was so limited that I assumed that all deviates were openly despised and rejected. Their grief and their fear drew my melancholy nature strongly. At first I only wanted to wallow in their misery, but, as time went by, I longed to reach its very essence. Finally I desired to represent it. By this process I managed to shift homosexuality from being a burden to being a cause. The weight lifted and some of the guilt evaporated.

It seemed to me that there were few homosexuals in the world. I felt that the entire strength of the club must be prepared to show its membership card at any time, and, to a nature as dramatic as mine, not to deny rapidly became to protest. By the time I was twenty-three I had made myself into a test case. I realized that it did no good to be seen to be homosexual in the West End where sin reigned supreme or in Soho which was inhabited exclusively by other outcasts of various kinds, but the rest of England was straightforward missionary country. It was densely populated by aborigines who had never heard of homosexuality and who, when first they did, became frightened and angry. I went to work on them.

The message I wished to propagate was that effeminacy existed in people who were in all other respects just like home. I went about the routine of daily living looking undeniably like a homosexual person. I had had a lot of practice at school in being the one against the many but, even so, I was not prepared for the effect my appearance had on the great British public. I had to begin cautiously.

I was from birth an object of mild ridicule because of my movements – especially the perpetual flutter of my hands – and my voice. Like the voices of a number of homosexuals, this is an insinuating blend of eagerness and caution in which even such words as 'Hallo' and 'Goodbye' seem not so much uttered as divulged. But these natural outward and visible signs of inward and spiritual disgrace were not enough. People could say that I was ignorant of them or was trying without success to hide them. I wanted it to be known that I was not ashamed and therefore had to display symptoms that could not be thought to be accidental.

I began to wear make-up. For a while I still went on as before at home and never mentioned to my mother anything about the life I lived in the outer world. She once protested that I never brought home any of my friends. I explained, quite truthfully, that she would hate them if I did. She never mentioned the matter again, which I took to be a sign that the protest was formal and that secretly she would be glad to hear no more on that subject.

Once outside the flat, I hurried like a wrong hushed up to the nearest public lavatory and put on my war-paint. Then I proceeded calmly wherever I was going. If I wasn't going anywhere, I tried to look as though I was. It became harder and harder to think of places to go and things to do as it slowly dawned on me that sex was definitely out – a realization that usually leaves people with a lot of spare time. If I was to become Miss Arc's only rival, it wouldn't do to allow myself to be picked up by strange men. This would give people the opportunity to say that I had only adopted an effeminate appearance for this purpose. Actually, from the moment that I began to look really startling, men ceased to make propositions to me. They found it too risky or too distasteful. But even the idea that this might be my intention must be eliminated. I began to walk faster and learned never to look strangers in the eye. Frequently in the street I swept past people I knew quite well. I once did this to my brother. This was just as well. He was with a girl who said, 'Did you see that?', to which he replied, 'Yes. Matter of fact, I've seen it before.'

Without knowing it, I was acquiring that haughty bearing which is characteristic of so many eccentrics. What other expression would you expect to find on the face of anyone who knows that if he turns his head too quickly, he will see on the faces of others glares of stark terror or grimaces of hatred? Aloofness is the posture of self-defence but even people who quite liked me said that I felt superior to the rest of the world. I felt scared and before long I was to have good cause.

By constantly complaining that the Battersea flat was sunless, my mother induced my father to buy a house outside High Wycombe. I could not do otherwise than go with them. My sister was by this time married; one of my brothers was abroad and the other was soon to go. Abroad was thought in those days to have some special advantages for young men of the middle classes and in this connection the word 'scope' was on everybody's lips. As in childhood I had evinced so much distaste for even going outside the front door, my parents made little attempt to send me overseas. In this they were very wise. I don't hold with abroad and think that foreigners speak English when our backs are turned.

Even High Wycombe to me was like a desert at the edge of civilization. As I roamed the fields adjacent to the house, forced by my mother to take her chow for a walk, between the hedges my starved eyes would see mirages of the London Pavilion or the Marble Arch and I would stumble towards them with little cries. My great fear was that here I might live and die and not matter. Just how distasteful my life was at this time cannot have been apparent to others. A friend of my sister, rushing in where even devils would have feared to tread, remarked, 'I wonder what you'd have been like if you'd been a woman. I suppose you'd have lived in the country and kept a dog and played bridge.' I was too choked with fury to be able to defend myself against this charge. Among other objections to this image of me was the fact that I hated animals. I still do. I have enough dumb friends without them.

In childhood I had longed to be taught dancing but nothing ever came of this. In a characteristic fit of indulgence my mother went so far as to buy me a pair of blocked ballet shoes (she did not know or care that no male dancer, except Mr Dolin in *Train Bleu*, had ever worn such things) but she never dared to mention to my father the idea of my becoming a dancer. It would have made him difficult to deal with for days. After the failure of journalism, she hammered away at commercial art as the last door through which it might be possible to push me into the outer world. I was sent to an art school in High Wycombe.

I had already done one term at Battersea Polytechnic before we left London and there had drawn a frog that the principal had thought was a piece of drapery. I don't think that I was taught anything. The only good that came of my attendance at this school was my meeting there with a girl who was to remain my friend for more than twenty years. She had been crippled by polio and wore a metal splint on one leg. At every step the whole side of her body had to be swung forward by a great effort from the shoulder. Despite this she was determined not to be left out of things. Her willpower was formidable. Because of her handicap, she was sympathetic to all deformity and was especially drawn to anyone she felt to be worse off than she. I came into this category.

The school at High Wycombe was, naturally, further out of touch with reality than the one in Battersea. Furniture design was well taught there because the town was the home of that industry which many years later formulated the 'G' plan. All other subjects were thought to be rather beside the point. None of the three or four men who comprised the staff had ever worked in an advertising agency or made free-lance commercial art into a paying profession. They would have been secretly ashamed to do so. Advertising was considered in those days a disgraceful trade. As no one felt confident to teach or even control me, I did more or less as I liked.

'What are you going to do this morning?'

'Oh, I don't know. A poster.'

'What of?'

'Coty's Ashes of Roses.' All my posters were exotic.

I very much doubt if, at the end of such a piece of dialogue as this, I was shown any advertising that M. Coty had recently put out, or, if I was, that I was warned that I must follow closely the existing line. I was encouraged to be original with some very far-fetched results. As I was now twenty-one and in a class full of girls in gym slips, I seemed by comparison a genius and behaved like one. I went to school, as one might say, in mufti, but my hair and my fingernails were long enough to cause comment from strangers on the way there and back.

Chapter Five

My father hated me chiefly because I was revolting but also because I was expensive. Sometimes he would turn on me at the dinner table and hiss, 'Don't eat so much butter on your bread.' To such injunctions I paid even less heed than usual for our life now seemed to be luxurious. I have since decided that with the move out of London my father had abandoned common sense altogether and plunged into a financial gamble that in his own way he was shortly to win.

We occupied what I would now call a very ordinary four-bedroom house and employed a housemaid and a gardener. This last feature of opulence was due not so much to the size of the garden as to the fact that nothing would have induced me to till or even to scratch the soil. I don't hold with flowers even when they are as good as artificial ones.

We also had a car but this could hardly be looked upon as a status symbol. Every car that my father bought was broken-down. He chose them like this deliberately so that he could spend almost all the week-end in the garage repairing them. This was a way of avoiding being with his family. Man goes and buys a car and lies beneath. When he was not tinkering with it, he was making the car the subject of one of our recurring Strindberg dramas. Every Sunday afternoon he asked my mother if she would like to go for a drive. She, who had learned her lines perfectly, said that she would.

'Where would you like to go?'

My mother then ploughed her way conscientiously through the list of places that were within driving distance. She was told that they were too far away or at the top or bottom of hills that were bad for the car. Then she was allowed to say, 'Well, anywhere. I don't mind.'

'If you don't care where we go,' my father would conclude, 'we might as well stay at home.'

But we didn't and the whole afternoon was hell.

About eighteen months after we moved to High Wycombe, the dreary ritual of our lives was interrupted by my mother going away for a few days. What caused this to happen, I can't remember. Perhaps she left in self-defence. This was a very rare occurrence as neither my father nor I could boil a kettle unless conditions were favourable. This was further evidence of the rigid sexual structure of the world at this time. Men fetched coal from cellars and hammered nails; women boiled kettles. You knew where you were even though you hated it.

My father and I got on shakily but, to my amazement, not badly. We spoke to each other. He asked me what I intended to do with my life and at last I understood that the future was now. Neither of my parents ever said to me, 'You're mad but, when you go out into the world, you will doubtless meet people as mad as you and I can only hope that you get on all right with them.' Such words as these would have been a great help. Instead, my mother protected me from the world and my father threatened me with it. My feeling of inadequacy increased steadily. I remember a day when my mother and I stood beside the road at Loudwater station and waited for my father to emerge from the London train. As we stood there, a stream of men in dark suits and bowler hats went by us. I thought, 'I'll never be able to get into step with them.' I

39

felt as I had in childhood when two other children turned a skipping-rope and urged me to run under it and start jumping. I couldn't do it.

Hateful was the dark-blue serge . . . O, why should life all labour be? Perhaps I was a born lotus-eater suffering from permanent symptoms of withdrawal.

At the end of one of the ominous but not hostile conversations with my father that took place during my mother's absence, he said, 'The trouble is you look like a male whore.'

This cheered me up a little as I had not then taken my final vows. I was in a twilit state between sin and virtue. The remark was the first acknowledgment that he had ever made of any part of my problem. In gratitude I promised that when I went up to London at Christmas, I would try not to come back.

Chapter Six

❧

At the Black Cat (which by this time honoured me by turning me out) there had been one young man who had come in for a certain amount of notoriety by boasting that he was not on the game. In proof of this claim he carried books under his arm and occasionally snubbed the other members of the clientèle with snippets of literature – chiefly by Michael Arlen. He was the least likeable of the lot. It was inevitably him that I got to know best. Being at the losing end of human relationships does not necessarily mean that you are perpetually climbing towards a vanishing ideal. After a while your despondency may bring you to a halt where you can be overtaken by absolutely anyone who wishes to know you. If I was standing still and he was reaching up to me, he must have come from depths that only Dante could calculate. I didn't think of this. He was the only person of my own age whom I knew well and who lived by himself in London. Whenever I had saved up enough pocket money to pay the fare from High Wycombe, I went to stay with him for week-ends. Once I even allowed myself to be nagged into inviting him for a day or two to my parents' house. He was short with black hair ending in a staccato manner at the back and his thumbnails were wider than they were long. When my mother saw them she made the special face that people make when they hear a knife skidding across a tin plate. She was very good at this expression. Towards the end of her life, she went into it whenever fingernails were even mentioned. She was half-way there by nature, having a high bridge to her nose, hooded eyes and lips that were made for sucking a lemon.

When the time came for me to leave home for good, with a red handkerchief full of cosmetics tied to a birch rod over my shoulder, it was towards these thumbnails that I turned my steps. The world lay all before me – like a trap-door.

In letters so voluminous that the postman scarcely had strength to deliver them, we had made our plans. My friend had taken a flat in Baron's Court, which we shared for three months. He seemed genuinely pleased that we were going to live together. I am so constituted that if I am told someone does not like me, I say, 'Why?' but, if I am told that they do, I only put my head on one side and lower my eyelids. I therefore never asked myself what on earth this man hoped to gain by setting up house with me. We were not lovers and soon we were not friends, but he never told me to go, though within weeks it transpired that I was a dead loss. I had no capacity to survive. He had probably guessed that if our lot was to be improved he would have to drag me forward, but after living with me for a week, he knew that if our affairs were merely to stay the same he would have to hold me up.

He had visited my home and seen that I was invincibly middle-class or worse (my mother had a faint cockney accent), but I may have seemed to him to be of high degree. Perhaps he thought that one day something must come of all the talents I claimed by implication to possess. I never stopped quoting my own stories, plays and poems. If he did think this, it would have carried great weight, for what Mr Haggard was to me, Mr Arlen was to him. He lived in an all-pervading dream about the well-born, the well-paid and the well-publicized. About the worship of talent and fame there is something gay and forward-looking.

A neophyte may one day achieve some measure of these things for himself but I can never help flinching from a display of undue reverence for titles. It seems so hopeless and self-wounding. This young man fell upon the thorns of class; he bled. Nothing would induce him, he once told me, to have his shoes cleaned in the street. It was such a cruel display of the master-servant relationship. When we were camping, one sunny day, with some men laying pipes in Hyde Park, he was shattered because one of the workmen said of a roll of putty that he was manipulating, 'The more you play with it, the longer it gets. It's like a navvy's prick.' While I was trying to pretend that I had not heard this affront to my maidenly modesty, Thumbnails was recovering from the pain of having heard a labourer pierce himself to the heart by calling himself a 'navvy'.

For whatever prestige he hoped my companionship would bring him my companion paid a punishing price. It was 1931. I had no job and most of the time he had none. We were driven to some dodgy expedients, and he had not only to run risks on my behalf but also to put up with my unconcealed disgust for the methods by which he provided food that my moral compunction never prevented me from eating. As we all know from witnessing the consuming jealousy of husbands who are never faithful, people do not confine themselves to the emotions to which they are entitled.

Our great money-saving device was used on the chain teashops – A.B.C., Lyons, etc. We patronized them (or should I say they patronized us?) only during rush hours, going in separately but sitting together. We ate fast so as not to use up all the rush hour and asked for separate bills so that we could leave one at a time. We took it in turns to go first. Whoever did this went to the pay desk and changed sixpence into coppers to make a telephone call so that the manageress would see him speak to the cashier. If he was challenged, he said his friend was paying. Whoever remained behind could try anything. He could pass the cash desk in the crowd; he could say his friend had paid; he also could ask for pennies to make a telephone call, but against this move there would in any chess book be a bracketed question-mark; he could pay his own bill; or he could admit defeat and pay both. This almost never happened. In six months, we nearly always ate one or two free meals a day.

I did not object to these felonies because they were against the law. My very existence was illegal. I was embarrassed by their pettiness and cross because, if I were apprehended in connection with any of them, the snow-white brand image of a homosexual person, towards which I had begun intermittently to work, would be dimmed. So far, however, I couldn't really afford virtue so I settled for indignation with vice. It served roughly the same purpose and was much cheaper.

While I was still living in Baron's Court, my father won his great gamble with the future. He died. On hearing of the death of anyone I have known well, I have usually experienced a slight thrill of pleasure. Another witness to my stupidity or weakness has been silenced. When the telegram announcing my father's death arrived, I felt nothing except irritation at the thought of having to go home, attend the funeral and come back. Though I loathed my life in London, I knew that this was what I must do. If I stayed away, the same nagging from my family would begin all over again. Not that I was free from being nagged in London. Indeed reprimands constituted almost the whole of my flat-mate's discourse – especially when we were in public. While we sat in the various teashops or walked along the streets, smiling and nodding so as to seem to strangers to be talking airily of this and that, he was saying, 'You

44

look terrible. Push your hair back from your forehead. Not abruptly as though I had mentioned it. Casually. That's a bit better. And for God's sake don't look so crushed. Smile.' This kind of nagging I hardly minded at first. It made everything I did or said or looked a matter of importance, but, as feelings of hunger, hopelessness and hatred began to weaken even my interest in myself, I started to long to get away. Freedom did not come for six months. Before then my talent for attracting public ridicule was to be put to the greatest test so far. I went on the stage.

One evening, Thumbnails, introducing himself as a journalist, arrived in the dressing-room of the speciality dancer of a pantomime in Hammersmith. One of her numbers had included a few hit-or-miss *fouettés*. He told her that if, on a given night, she were to do thirty-two of these steps, it would constitute a record and be worth mentioning in the papers.

On the night in question the pantomime dancer, in fact, shuddered to a halt after barely beginning her marathon, but journalism, like the Light of Lights, looks on the motive not the deed, and the story was printed just the same. When the papers came out everybody kissed everybody and the dancer was so grateful that she allowed herself to be persuaded to take part in a charity matinée at the Scala Theatre, in aid of some hospital or other. In order to stay on stage for more than a two-minute solo (which she fully intended to do, for her charity towards hospitals must not be doubted), the dancer explained that she must have a partner to wave his arms while she changed her costume and got her breath back. My flat-mate assured her that he knew just the person for the job.

Except for fighting with my little friend on the stage of Sutton Town Hall and playing the part of a madman in High Wycombe amateur theatricals, I had had no previous

45

stage experience whatsoever but, by this time, my whole life was an unsympathetic part played to a hostile audience. I felt that I had already done sufficient basic training. For the part of the act that involved me, the dancer had decided to do an acrobatic solo that she knew by heart with me as sort of visible stage hand. This number showed her as an idol enthroned on an altar and me as a slave – the oriental equivalent of a church brass cleaner. With matters arranged thus a few sketchy rehearsals were thought to be sufficient.

When the curtain went up on this part of the bill, I was revealed with my back to the audience in I can't remember whose pyjama trousers with my upper half sporadically coated with 'slave white'. I looked like an insufficiently basted chicken. As I moved one arm commanding a second layer of curtains to part, there was a deafening roar of laughter. I took this calmly. To me it was just like Piccadilly Circus. My partner must have been a bit surprised. She went bravely on, however, twisting, turning, writhing while I ran about the stage or clung to her for support, liberally streaking her unattainable whiteness with my orange make-up. As long as I was moving, the audience kept on laughing. When the curtain came down, we could have continued to bow until our discs slipped. The audience would have applauded for ever.

Chapter Seven

❧

By this time my companion and I were living in King's Cross, a much more fertile region than the one we had just left. Baron's Court had been a no-man's-land in which the houses were blind with stained glass and, on the pavements, raw trees no thicker than your arm stood in strait-jackets of chicken-wire wincing at every breath of wind. Our new location was loud with the noise of steam trains and lousy with teashops that had a well-defined rush hour.

Things were better without, but they had grown worse within. We now shared a double room for which the rent was eleven shillings each and we were almost never apart. My room-mate's idea of companionship included having me sit on the edge of the bath while he cleaned his teeth. My aversion caused me to live in a state of tension every moment that I was not alone, but the middle-class morality in which I had been so carefully reared prevailed. I hissed but I almost never shouted. I don't expect that this self-restraint would have lasted indefinitely but it didn't have to. After three months in King's Cross, news reached me from my mother which broke the siege.

My mother had a genius for making and keeping friends. This talent was instinctive and was exercised without a hope of profit. It was merely my good fortune that at least twice she was able to turn it to my account. The woman who many years before had introduced us to Mrs Longhurst now, for my mother's sake, persuaded one of the directors of a vast firm of consulting electrical engineers to give me employment. I was absolutely amazed. He paid me £2 10s. a week for eighteen months before coming to his senses. Until I had been in work long enough to become eligible for the dole (15s. 3d. a week) I almost held my breath. After that point was passed, my relief became evident in my general demeanour and particularly in the returning length of my hair and my fingernails.

Even greater than my joy at the prospect of one day being able to draw unemployment insurance was my ecstasy at moving into a room of my own. Once I had achieved this I was happy. All the reactions that other people have described to me when at last they found someone to live with – the heightened perception of the world around them, the inability to refrain from taking little skips as they walked – all these were mine on realizing that I might with luck never have to live with anyone again.

I was happy. The room I took (and even this I couldn't find without the help of the room-mate I was so gladly leaving) was in darkest Pimlico. It had Nottingham lace curtains at the window, corned beef linoleum on the floor and a brass bedstead in one corner. Some of my friends said how lucky I was to have been let in, while others laughed the room to scorn and implored me to chi-chi it up. I didn't listen. I was happy.

At work I never once understood what I was doing. In theory I was employed as an engineer's tracer. This was one of the many kinds of work at which I could never hope to become proficient. Accuracy is alien to my nature. Many years later a woman asked me what a 'point' was. When I told her it was a seventy-second part of an inch, she said, 'But there isn't such a thing, really. Is there?' That is what I have always secretly thought. When I was given plans to trace, I copied the mistakes as well as the revisions and neither of them properly; when I was told to transfer the positions of electric pylons from one map to another, I did so with such a jolly laugh that construction men telephoned from distant shires to ask what on earth was going on at head office. If any housewife has a pylon among her rose bushes, if any country clergyman has a pylon sticking up through his church roof, if any borough surveyor has a pylon blocking his main thoroughfare, may she or he read here that I apologize. May it comfort them to know that I was happy.

When I was not at work, I sat in my room and wrote plays, poems, libretti, stories which were never to see the light of publication. The crippling weakness of all these works was that the ideas they sought to embody were far too highbrow for my sub-Tennysonian style. This is the main fault in all the writings that I have ever read in manuscript. The poverty from which I have suffered could be diagnosed as 'Soho' poverty. It comes from having the airs and graces of a genius and no talent. But I was happy.

On evenings when I felt that I could write no more I went to visit friends, boys from the cafés who had rooms in houses where no landladies fly, or girls with whom I had been at art school. The journey there and back I nearly always made on foot to show that I could. It was getting harder all the time.

Exhibitionism is like a drug. Hooked in adolescence I was now taking doses so massive that they would have killed a novice. Blind with mascara and dumb with lipstick, I paraded the dim streets of Pimlico with my overcoat wrapped round me as though it were a tailless ermine cape. I had to walk like a mummy leaving its tomb. At every step one foot had to land directly in front of the other. My knees ground together. After about a mile of walking thus, my trousers began to wear out between the knees; after two miles I began to wear out. Sometimes I wore a fringe so deep that it completely obscured the way ahead. This hardly mattered. There were always others to look where I was going.

As my appearance progressed from the effeminate to the bizarre, the reaction of strangers passed from startled contempt to outraged hatred. They began to take action. If I was compelled to stand still in the street in order to wait for a bus or on the platform of an Underground railway station, people would turn without a word and slap my face; if I was wearing sandals, passers-by took care to stamp on my toes; and once a crowd had started to follow me, it grew and grew until no traffic could pass down the road. If I didn't put a stop to this quickly, by getting on a bus or going into a shop, the police had to deal with it. Barging his way through the yelling crowd or coming at me from a side street, the constable would say, 'You again. Move on.' Then, turning on the rabble with raised arms, he would tell them that it was over – that there was nothing to see (both of which statements were untrue). In a weary voice, he would implore them to pass along the pavement. I was excited, exhausted and worried by these crowds but, because I had never yet been savaged by them, I was not frightened. Because I still believed that I could educate them, I was happy.

Chapter Eight

◇

Homosexuals have time for everybody. This is not only an instance of the known law that all outsiders are polite to insiders because at best they secretly revere them or at worst fear that they may one day need them. Homosexuals are sincerely interested. They will sit for hours on stairs while chars complain about their rheumatism; they will stand at street corners while postmen rage against the handwriting of correspondents; they will pay extra fares to hear conductors rail against their wives. Every detail of the lives of real people, however mundane it may be, seems romantic to them. Romance is that enchantment that distance lends to things and homosexuals are in a different world from the 'dead normals' with many light-years dark between. If by some chance an hour of pointless gossip makes fleeting reference to some foible, some odd superstition, some illogical preference that they find they share with the speaker, homosexuals are as amazed and delighted as an Earthman would be on learning that Martians cook by gas.

I have this lust for small talk. Nobody escapes my love. When I was not writing my interminable manuscripts or stalking the streets, I was scrabbling away with my bare hands at the hearts of all the people who couldn't get away. At this time my friends were few because of the difficulties attendant upon knowing me. Many I could never visit because they had resident husbands, fathers or landladies; others I could visit occasionally but not meet in public because it was too embarrassing. On the other hand there was a handful who hardly liked my company at all but loved to cling to my arm in the street and fracture themselves with merriment while housewives hissed and workmen spat upon the ground before my gilded toes.

All were welcome in my room in Denbigh Street. Among my visitors were the student from High Wycombe and the student from Battersea whose cousin, when alone with me, flung herself on the floor at my feet and said she wasn't worthy of me. This was true but I never understood why she brought the subject up. A male prostitute (re-named Greta on account of his reverence for Garbo) used to call, and a model whom I had met in Hyde Park who brought with him a Czech gentleman with an unspellable name. But my most faithful guests were an Irish boy, his friend who was a deserter from the Seaforth Highlanders and a girl who ran a shuttle service between them.

My friendship with the Irishman was a sexless variation on a well-known theme. I have no doubt that I met him at the Marble Arch. In those days there must have been a picture of this monument and a map of the surrounding streets on the wall of every gentlemen's lavatory in Cardiff, Glasgow, Belfast and points west, for whenever a ruined Celt arrived in London, this is where he came to rest – or should I say work? And the sort of man who liked that sort of thing could go there and pick one of these boys from the wall as though he were plucking a peach which, indeed, some of the specimens resembled.

If these down-and-outs were innocent when they arrived and merely stood about at Marble Arch in order to be with their countrymen, they soon learned to tap the steamers and before long to aim for the rich-looking homosexuals. It was especially the Irish who concentrated on these. They felt that with them they could run up and down the scales of flattery without a hint of *pianissimo*. Though they did this for venal ends, they also enjoyed it. It was the exercise of their native genius. As Italian is the language of song, Irish is the voice of flattery. From the lips of these young men I have heard phrases so archaic and hyperboles so florid that even Mr Synge could not have used them without a giggle. When they gave it up you knew they liked you. This was the stage in our friendship that the Irish boy and I had reached by the time he was my guest in Pimlico.

Though mercifully the flattery dies, the hard-luck story never fades. If I were asked what the word 'con' meant, I would say that it was something done by impecunious Irishmen to English queers.

So the reason why the Irishman, his friend and their girl called on me so often was because they were always in need of sixpence. Knowing someone poorer than myself when I only earned £2 10s. was a luxury and I usually tried to indulge myself as well as them. Their own description of the situation was that they 'tapped me unmercifully' but if I refused them a loan they never turned nasty, and when I gave them something I never asked for it to be returned or suggested that they should do anything to deserve it. In this way our friendship was kept pleasant for a great many years. It faded gracefully as time and the world intervened.

While I lived in Pimlico and worked at my first job, I did not reach that state of terrible gaiety that I was to achieve later. To some extent I still lived in the future – a habit which is the death of happiness. I wrote a play about Helen of Troy and looked forward to the day when it would be published along with a lot of other works. I still hoped to find tolerance for my kind and love for myself though I now saw that this could not be reached by means of sex. It would be less true to say that I saw through sex than to say that I no longer saw through it. It had ceased to be a door to a sustaining relationship. It had become its slightly distasteful self. For many years I was at least happy enough to live without sexual encounters at all. Sex is the last refuge of the miserable. All the same I indulged in fantasies of living the public life of a famous writer, painter or actor combined with the private life of a cleaned-up odalisque. When I switched these dreams off and came to terms with my true expectations, I could not avoid seeing that I was always going to have a very circumscribed life. If travelling to Ealing was like embarking on a crusade, I could be fairly sure that I was never going to Rome or Paris or New York; if it had taken me twenty-two years to crawl into a job that I could only do badly, I was never likely to live the briefcase life. I must not expect that I would ever have money or influence. I had better decide on some one small thing that I really wanted and aim to achieve some measure of that. I chose happiness and, like Bernard Shaw's serpent, I set about willing what I had imagined and creating what I had willed.

The essence of happiness is its absoluteness. It is automatically the state of being of those who live in the continuous present all over their bodies. No effort is required to define or even attain happiness, but enormous concentration is needed to abandon everything else.

Graham Greene has boasted that wherever we can show him happiness, he will show us ignorance, selfishness and greed. Had his words been written forty years ago, I would have known that much sooner that happiness was something for which I was naturally equipped. Unfortunately there are two other requirements – good health and solvency. The first of these prerequisites I have enjoyed

54

almost continuously since people ceased to look after me, but the second has failed me at several periods of my life. One such wave of penury was to engulf me within a week of leaving my job with the electrical engineers.

Chapter Nine

❧

When I was swept down into this second trough of destitution, I found myself in general worse off than when I had first come to London, but there were a few respects in which my lot was improved. I lived on my own. It is hard enough to share wealth without being involved in undignified scenes; shared poverty consists of nothing else. Alone, I could spread the little money I had to cover – or almost to cover – my vital needs and I could decide, without that irksome effort towards consistency which I always make in the presence of others, just which underhand dodges I would attempt and which were so risky as to be beneath me. After a while my morality came to rest at a level at which it has remained ever since. If I saw someone ahead of me in the street drop a pound note, I would overtake him and give it back, but if I found a pound note in the gutter and had no idea to whom it had belonged, I would certainly not take it to the nearest police station. I imagine most people come gradually to some completely illogical code of this kind and describe themselves as reasonably honest.

Another way in which things were now better than they had been in King's Cross was that, instead of receiving every week fourteen guilt-edged shillings from my mother, I drew fifteen shillings three pence from the taxpayers who, though they complained more, could afford it better. Getting the money was one of the ways in which life was harder.

The Pentonville Labour Exchange looked like a vast one-storey barn and issuing appropriately from it I always heard a bellowing sound. This was the noise which, as soon as I appeared on the horizon, was set up by the four-deep queue that permanently surrounded the building. The lowing was sustained *fortissimo* during the whole time that I was inside the building and only died away as I disappeared round the corner of the street. To such a din I was already more or less inured. What came as a shock was having what modern tube-travellers call the 'rush hour technique' practised in a spirit of mockery upon my person. While I was in the middle of the queue, both hands were fully occupied in fending off the fumblers who were busy fore and aft. It was a mercy that I was able to press my genital organs firmly against the counter at the moment when one hand had to be released for the purpose of signing the book. Only the eternal presence of two policemen, one at each door of the building, prevented a fight.

One day, after weeks of this ritual, a solemn but benign figure appeared on the other side of the counter and beckoned me. The tumult and the shouting died; the moving fingers left my fly-buttons. A clerk lifted up the flap of the counter and pointed towards the doorway through which the manager had receded. His office was very small and, apart from his own desk, crowded with at least three others. At these clerks sat with their heads bowed and their pens poised a fraction of an inch above their work. I do not think a single figure was written while I was in the room.

The ruler of the Labour Exchange motioned me to sit on a chair in front of his desk and began to address me in a magisterial but kindly voice. 'I came out to see what all the noise was about,' he said. 'I suppose you know it's on account of you.'

Me: Yes, sir.

Ruler: I see we have you down as an engineer's tracer. Do you think, looking as you do, that you are likely to get work of this kind?

Me: I would like to find work as a commercial artist.

While employed by the electrical firm I had attended evening classes in life drawing and illustration at the Regent Street Polytechnic. (The principal of St Martin's School of Art had refused to admit me, saying that it was a miracle that I had a job at all and that I had better not try to change it.) I now mentioned these studies in the hope of seeming serious-minded. I said it might be a little less unlikely that I would find work in a studio than in an office. My inquisitor agreed. He couldn't stop himself from asking why I had adopted such a peculiar appearance. Then not only the pens but the pulses of the surrounding clerks stood still.

Ruler: Why do you go about looking as you do?

Me: Because this is the way I am. I wouldn't like you or anyone else to think I was ashamed.

He must have been a truly enlightened man for, though we were still stumbling through the sexual darkness of 1933, he did not ask me what I meant. He said, 'I think you're making things very difficult for yourself.' Then he rose to his feet and I to mine. 'You had better go out by this door,' he added kindly, escorting me to a staff entrance. When I turned in the doorway to thank him he said, 'If it all gets too much for you, come and see me again. I will see what I can do.' As he uttered these words he placed his hand on my shoulder, a gesture which, in the circumstances, amounted to a daring vote of confidence. He was the first official ever to treat my problem as at least real to me.

The fifteen shillings three pence which through his beneficence I drew from the Labour Exchange for six months had to be eked out very carefully.

I took a room, the rent of which was six shillings a week,

in a Clerkenwell house which belonged to a superannuated policeman and his wife. They were type-cast. I could almost see on her hands the flour from the first pie with which she had lured her husband from his beat down the area steps into her kitchen. The attic which they let to me was long enough to lie down in but would not have been wide enough for that purpose and was too low to stand up in. A six-foot man would have died of lumbago. The furniture consisted of a bed as narrow as a coffin (though not as peaceful), beside which stood a washstand with a jug and basin on it. At the foot of the bed was a little table with a chair placed so that a man of no cubic capacity whatsoever could sit there. But not only could no one, however starved, have made use of the chair where it stood; he could also not sit on it anywhere else. It could not be extricated from its position without the whole place being dismantled. The room had a window through which I could squeeze myself on to the roof. Here in the bitter summer weather I used to lie on the foot-wide parapet that ran round the top of the house. I hoped I would go to sleep and fall into the street below. I never did. Even a cheap death is hard to come by.

After paying my rent, I had nine shillings three pence left, of which a shilling a day was spent on food. On week-days I could eat a midday meal for this amount in a dining-room near Euston Station. It was run by a big, blonde woman whose conversation was a sort of ad lib. trailer for *Coronation Street*. I used to go to her restaurant after the lunch hour crowd had left and before the food had had time to get cold. She gave me whatever food she wanted to get rid of, saying that all the other dishes written on the blackboard had not turned out very nice. 'Cut it on the bias,' she screamed down the service lift shaft to her husband. This he certainly did. At every meal I levelled to the ground two pyramids of food that would have daunted a Pharaoh.

Throughout my early life, the amount of food I ate was a cause for incessant criticism by my friends. At first I used to point out in a whimpering voice that most of my acquaintances only saw me in cafés where, since I sat in them from noon to nightfall and sometimes beyond, the least I could do to appease the proprietors was spend money. Later I grew tired of defending myself. I take it to be axiomatic that people are revolted by witnessing the shameless gratification of an appetite they do not share.

To this rule the proprietress of the one shilling diner-restaurant was an exception. If the place was empty she abandoned the work of clearing up to sit and watch me eat. Her kindness was an absolutely genuine emotion based on the snobbery of the times.

In spite of my astonishing disdain, I had still not succeeded in shaking off my former room-mate. This was just as well. He had discovered both the attic and the dining-room which now made my existence possible. We often ate together but, though his airs and graces were far less pronounced than mine, the proprietress did not like him. She fed him well but spoke of him badly. 'It's different with you, luv. But him! Why, some of the lads round here went to school with him.' She felt that he should have spoken the same language as they and not tried to deceive her into treating him with respect. This attempted imposture made him unworthy of extra helpings of jam roll. I have no way of knowing that she did not disparage me to him when he was there alone but, as far as I could see, she was pleased with me. I was a real gentleman. This by itself would have been but little recommendation. What mattered was that I was of high degree but at low ebb. Every ladleful of mashed potato that she sloshed on to my plate, in her heart she flung into the face of the existing social order. Not with impudence but with a kindness that not even Christ (the gentleman with the longest hard-luck story of them all) could disapprove, she became for a moment the superior of her superiors.

This attitude of mind was one of the two great snobberies by which I was amazed to find that I could profit. The second was the common man's reverence for the arts.

Art, by which the people who used the word always meant painting, was in those days sacred. It had not yet fallen into disrepute by becoming a game that any number could play. It was not a profession by which a great deal of money could be made. It was still a divine madness which caused the possessed to grow their hair long and lead lives of unalleviated poverty. Once, when I fainted in an Express Dairy, the manageress almost carried me downstairs to a part of the restaurant that was not used in the evenings. There she fed me with her own hand as though I were a pigeon – only rarer. 'You're an artist, I expect,' she murmured. 'You don't always remember to have regular meals.' I gave a wan smile of gratitude and, touched by her sweetness, paid my bill.

Later, when I lived in Chelsea (which was proof positive that I was not of this world), this deference to art often saved my skin. As I stood pressed against the railings of some dim London square with a stranger's hand at my throat or my crutch or both, another member of the gang would whisper, 'But he's an artist. I seen him in Chelsea.' Immediately the grip on my person would loosen and, in a shaken voice, my aggressor would say, 'I didn't know.'

The art that I practised at this time consisted of re-arranging the position of the words 'Sea View' on the letterhead of some boarding house in Brighton. This it did not seem necessary to mention.

When I had eaten my sixth huge meal of the week in the dining-room by Euston Station, there was, in theory (if no disaster such as having to buy a piece of soap had overtaken me), three shillings three pence left for buying Sunday dinner. When, many years after this time, a friend of mine went to Israel to keep house for a doctor, she wrote and asked if I knew of any recipes that required no stove and no food. I couldn't help her, and I couldn't help myself when I lived in Clerkenwell. I had no idea how to live cheaply. I used to buy a loaf of bread, a pint of milk and a hunk of black chocolate so hard that the confectioner could only break it with a small axe which possibly he kept solely for this purpose. These provisions I consumed lying on my bed, which I seldom left for the whole week-end (unless lured out by other people's food). It is easier to starve supine than erect.

That was how I spent Saturday and Sunday when things had gone well. Quite often I had by this time already been bullied by the local boys into parting with several pennies or, worse, a sixpence. Even those who had seen me at the Labour Exchange were not above begging from me.

In spite of my intense interest in these men I never came fully to comprehend the attitude they adopted towards me and my kind. This may partly have been because I feared and desired and sentimentalized them. It may also not have been their intention that I should understand them. If I was busy trying to seem mysterious and aloof to them, we must not rule out the possibility that they were reciprocally engaged.

This denomination of the homosexual religion is quasi-normal, and the same exaggerated and over-simplified distinction that separated men from women in the outer world ran like a wall straight and impassable between the 'roughs' and the 'bitches'. I was over thirty before, for the first time, I heard somebody say that he did not think of himself as masculine or feminine but merely as a person attracted to other persons with male sexual organs. A confession of this nature would still bewilder and, perhaps, anger some of my homosexual friends. Quite recently a male prostitute of my acquaintance, on one of his amateur nights, picked up a young soldier only to find at the crucial moment that he had lumbered himself with a passive sodomite. 'And, all of a sudden, he turned over. After all I'd done – flitting about the room in my wrap, making him coffee. You know, camping myself silly. My dear, I was disgusted. I made him get up and put on his clothes again.' Whether he did in fact make the soldier get out of bed the instant the awful discovery was made is beside the point. The speaker wished all those who heard this tale to appreciate how clear a moral distinction there was between him and certain other people to whom sex is a mere pleasure mechanism. This point would have been understood immediately by the homosexuals I knew in my Clerkenwell days.

They were all pseudo-women in search of pseudo-men. To this idea the roughs undoubtedly pandered, either permanently because it was part of some self-congratulatory idea they had of themselves, or temporarily whenever they were with us. They consciously tried to embody the myth of the great dark man which haunts the dreams of pathological homosexuals and is the cause of one of their dilemmas.

This problem is similar to the one that confronts heterosexuals who happen to be ever so for virgins.

Recently a letter was published in one of the women's papers asking how the writer should deal with her young man. He had told her that he would only happily marry a virgin. He pointed out that he could not possibly know for certain that she was pure unless he had sexual intercourse with her. This letter may, in fact, have been written by the editor but it poses a riddle that men are only slowly ceasing to try to solve. The parallel problem that confronts homosexuals is that they set out to win the love of a 'real' man. If they succeed, they fail. A man who 'goes with' other men is not what they would call a real man. This conundrum is incapable of resolution, but that does not make homosexuals give it up. They only search more frantically and with less and less discretion for more and more masculine men and because they themselves are, however reluctantly, to some extent masculine their judgment in these matters is for the most part physical. If you ask a homosexual what his newest true love is like, you will never get the answer, 'He is wise or kind or brave.' He will only say, 'It's enormous.'

Though, in the heterosexual world of the 'twenties and 'thirties, masculinity was sacred, the brand image of it had not come to its fullest flower in the minds of women. Their heroes were Rudolph Valentino and, later, Ivor Novello. It would have been delightful to know how the latter spoke in private of the parts which in public he played with such dash. In one play, to show how virile he was, he spat a piece of apple he was chewing on to the floor before demanding a kiss from a wicked woman in a low café in Montmartre.

Wicked Woman: But we don't love each other, do we?
Mr Novello: What the hell do we care! (*They kiss.*)
Curtain.

This was masculinity stalking towards the deliciously quivering stalls.

Another thing that may have prevented women from coming out openly in favour of unretouched masculinity was that love and marriage in those days were still confused in their minds. They could only stretch out one hand towards the untamed male. With the other they were preventing the escape of someone whom they regarded

64

as a suitable husband – a person of the same class, size, age and nationality as they. Homosexuals do not need to divide their attention in this troublesome way. They can clutch with both hands at the myth of the great dark man. Their choice, unless they suffer from some subsidiary kink, is guided by the desire to bolster up, with a number of contrasts, that dream of themselves which it is their one increasing purpose to maintain.

To understand what kind of man they most admire it is only necessary to guess what they wish they themselves were – young, frail, beautiful and refined. Hence their predilection is for huge, violent, coarse brutes.

Any of these characteristics that the roughs did not possess by nature, they could put on at a moment's notice as mating plumage. But they, too, had a problem.

The exotic had for them a great lure based on its rarity. The idea of the orchidaceous woman was everywhere. Greta Garbo and Marlene Dietrich leaned down from the screen and shamelessly poured sequins over the heads of the one-and-ninepennies, but from the real lives of working-class men this element was almost totally lacking. The girls available to them were just like home. Parents in those days still had some say in what their daughters wore. Only prostitutes at that social level wore vermilion hair, gold eyelids and green fingernails. The girl next door had to make a necessity of virtue.

Men appeared to go along with this idea but it was noticeable that, whenever pansies were in bloom, they couldn't resist doing a little window shopping. They must never admit to themselves or to God or to one another that they even liked the company of homosexuals – let alone that 'trade' with them was a pleasurable pastime. Any attention that they paid to us had to be put in the form of an infliction. Such gestures as running their fingers through our hair were accompanied by insults about what a bloody awful mop it was. If they wished to make any more definitely sexual advances, these must be ruthlessly stripped of any quality of indulgence. I have known at least one heterosexual man who told me that, to be really satisfactory, all sexual intercourse must preserve the illusion of rape, so I was never able to decide how much of the inordinate interest taken in me by the Clerkenwell boys was due to sexual curiosity and how much was what it seemed – hatred. I longed to know, but I soon had to deprive myself of the strong stimulus that their proximity provided. The danger was too great.

Keeping out of their way was not easy for topographical reasons. A partial solution to the problem of how to avoid trouble at the hands of roughs would have been never to go out at a time when decent people were in their beds. Decency, however, must be an even more exhausting state to maintain than its opposite. Those who succeed seem to need a stupefying amount of sleep. Even by ten o'clock at night the streets of all the slum districts I ever lived in were empty of every living thing but toughs. To reach home at all after this hour I had to pass some of them.

The shortest route between the strictly comparative safety of the main road and my front door lay to the north, but this was the most densely populated part of the neighbourhood. Therefore in a sense it was the most dangerous. If I had recently met with any trouble there, I used to try coming home through the quieter area to the south by walking up Rosebery Avenue and nipping into any of the dark turnings on the left when I judged that I was not being watched. The disadvantage of this plan was that, unless I went a very long way round indeed, I had to pass at the corner of Farringdon Road a coffee stall round which there was always a crowd of young men.

One night, when I had just risked this hazard, I became

aware that I was being followed by more than one person. I was in trouble.

I lived every moment that I was out of doors in a state of feverish awareness. It covered only a limited area of human experience. Outside the field of my own safety I was the least observant person. I could never give people correct street directions nor describe places with any accuracy, even if they were landmarks that I passed every day, but if I heard strangers walking along the road behind me, I knew at once whether they just happened to be there or whether they were pursuers. I could usually gauge how many members of the hunt were present even though they might all be marching in step precisely for the purpose of deceiving me on this point. I could tell if there was a woman among them. The presence of a girl almost always meant that the situation was going to be less grim.

Once I had made up my mind about all these details, there were automatically a number of rules that must be followed. I must never look back; I must on no account run but must increase my rate of progress gradually. A pace of more than four miles an hour eliminates half-hearted murderers. Serious ones will, at this point, break into a run. You will then know for certain that your predicament is of the worst kind.

Even when overtaken and addressed (with some such words as 'Who the hell do you think you are?'), I seldom ceased to walk fast until I was forcibly stopped. Then I would stand absolutely still and look at the person holding my arm. Sometimes a look (which must never be haughty) was enough to make them let go of my sleeve. If it was not, I would try an offer of money, whether they asked me for any or not. As of necessity the amount proffered was small, my aggressors frequently knocked it out of my hand. I was left with no other pacifying strategy than speech. I spoke very slowly and very quietly. This had the effect of compelling my enemies to listen but it was at best only a delaying tactic. While I talked, they remained silent if only to enjoy the luxury of hearing themselves called 'Sir'. But even I could not prolong a filibuster indefinitely. As soon as I paused for breath or by mistake asked a question, they started to work themselves into a frenzy by shouting, swearing and laughing – a device that I am told is standard procedure in bayonet practice.

One night this ritual had just begun when a taxi came down the street. I raised my arm and to my amazement the taxi stopped, but as soon as I got into it and the boys began to surge round, the driver realized what the situation was and, getting down from his seat, ordered me out of his cab. This was not what always happened. I have on other similar occasions known a taxi-driver to run considerable risk to himself and his vehicle by moving slowly but persistently forward through dense crowds that hammered with their fists on the sides of the cab while inside I pulled, as though they were reins, at the leather straps which in those days held the windows of taxis shut.

The taxi-driver in Rosebery Avenue, either from caution or moral indignation, had no intention of making a gesture in my favour. He stood in the road and continued to demand that I get out. This I did not immediately do. One of the boys started to drag me out. It was foolish of me to allow this to happen as, by resisting, I became part of the battle. As soon as I was in the street once more, the whole gang started to hit me from all sides. Almost immediately I fell on to my hands and knees in the gutter. For a second, I wondered whether I could stay there for ever, but, fearing that I might be kicked, I staggered to my feet and was at once knocked across the pavement by a single, more carefully aimed blow. As I leaned against the front of Finsbury Town Hall covering my own equally ornate façade with my hands to try to prevent rivers of mascara from running down my cheeks, I said, 'I seem to have annoyed you gentlemen in some way.'

At this there was a sound of genuine amusement quite unlike the barking noise emitted by a lynching party. I knew that this was the moment to try to move away though I could hardly see where I was going. As I lurched along the wall, voices shouted after me but no one followed. Apparently whatever point my enemies had wished to make had been established.

The mysterious thing in all such occurrences was not that strangers, sometimes without a word being uttered on either side, attacked me. It was that they never killed me. Certainly fear did not restrain them. I never made even a pretence of defending myself (not because my behaviour was modelled on Christian ethics but because to try would only have provoked redoubled ferocity from my aggressors), and no one ever came to my aid. Also, these young men must have known that whatever they did to me, there would have been only the most perfunctory police inquiry into the incident, yet though on two occasions I have lain for a few seconds unconscious on the pavement, I was never damaged beyond repair. My assailants did not apparently require my death nor even my disfigurement. This was why I concluded that a large part of their motive for attacking me was to release their sexual curiosity in a manner consistent with their heavily guarded idea of manliness. They were only slightly concerned with forcing me to accept their superiority. If this latter was their whole aim, then all those street brawls were a waste of time. I regarded all heterosexuals, however low, as superior to any homosexual, however noble.

Chapter Ten

❧

This skirmish must have occurred towards the end of my stay in Clerkenwell. By this time I was once again in a job. I remember that I had difficulty in forcing myself to go to work the following day. This was not because I felt ill. To my surprise I found, when I awoke the next morning, that I was not suffering even from the slightest headache. My reluctance to step outside the front door was due to the fact that when I looked in the looking glass (which I did the moment I was fully conscious) I saw that one side of my face was an ashy grey and the other the colour of blackberry juice. I ought not to have worried about the comment that this might cause in the office. I should have known that I could rely on the Englishness of the English. No one said a word. This was probably not from lack of curiosity. One of the travellers for this firm told me that when the directors had given him lunch in the public house next door, the sole topic of conversation had been 'whether I did or whether I didn't'. Nevertheless they would have died rather than hear any of the details of my private life from my own two lips. They guessed – and they were right – that if they questioned me at all, no matter how flippantly, they would have had the whole truth forced upon them.

This new job, like my first, was found for me by my mother. Digging ever deeper through older and older strata of friendship, she had unearthed the wife of a publisher whom we had all known in Sutton. (I had been to one of their hateful parties during which, rather than play games in which somebody had to kiss somebody, I had sat in another room and played patience with cards which I had had the forethought to bring with me.) My mother, in a fragment of the voluminous correspondence which, now that she lived in farthest Devonshire, was her chief hobby, pleaded with this woman, who nagged her husband, who coerced a printing firm with whom he did a lot of business, to employ me in their art department.

I was not a success. I sat in an upper room and tried to adapt myself to the whims of a man so moody that most days passed in a silence unbroken even by greeting or valediction. On others he danced and sang with such vigour that, even if there had been any work to which my talents were equal, I could not have done it. The swinging of the lamps and the shaking of the floor would have prevented me. Some of his moodiness was, I think, due to his red hair but more was caused by the burden that he carried on my behalf. As the head of our department, one of his duties was to take whatever work I did downstairs to the directors and explain it if he could. Doing this always brought down upon him humiliations that he could hardly bear. As a commercial artist, I was as hopeless as I had been as a tracer. Indeed, the qualifications were the same for both occupations – a slow pulse, good eyesight and a minimum of ideas. The word 'slick', now a term of contempt, was then the highest praise. In all the long dark years that I was in or on the fringe of advertising, my work never attained any noticeable degree of this quality of high gloss. I was always compelled to spend hours retouching my lettering and hours more retouching the retouching until the paper was embossed with white paint. The words I had written could only be read by the blind.

After a year of watching me doing this, the red-haired

artist gave notice. As he left he said, 'I feel I ought to say something – give you some advice – but the thing for you to do is to carry on just the way you do now. You're as meek as a bloody lamb but down there (he jerked his fifteen-amp hair towards the floor, meaning in the board room – not in hell) they know you don't care a damn about any of them and there's just nothing they can do about it.'

He was wrong. I liked the directors; I had arranged to do so. I was secretly shocked to see stalking towards me naked what, in my first job, I had only seen heavily veiled – the senseless and implacable hatred that workers feel for their employers. This hostility was something to which I never grew accustomed. In my whole life, the only relationships with individuals (as opposed to crowds) that I took seriously were those that I managed to establish with the people for whom I worked. They paid me and this raised them higher in my esteem than any amount of praise or protestation of affection ever could. In return I was their slave. To the amazement and sometimes the disgust of my co-workers in various studios I never attempted to introduce any quality into my work that might be over the head of my boss. Nay, I executed drawings that I knew to be of the utmost banality with positive gusto, for whatever is done for money is sacred.

For the first three months in the printing firm, my employers and I were only engaged – not actually married. Explaining that I was on approval, they paid me nothing. Three times a week I was given permission to walk across London (it would have been madness to have spent a penny each way on fares) and sign on at the Labour Exchange. This was but one of the bewildering flashes in which the dark core of the mind of accountancy was revealed to me.

On one of the many days on which there was little that I could profitably do sitting at my desk, I was sent out to buy a pair of scissors. I went to Selfridge's department store, which I felt that I understood. It was thence that my tuck had been sent to me at boarding school. I bought some scissors for five shillings. When I returned and told the girl who kept the petty cash book how much they had cost, she became distraught. 'I can't put down "Scissors, five shillings",' she wailed. 'You can buy a pair in Woolworth's for sixpence.' I tried to calm her by enumerating the ways in which the article I had bought was superior to anything sold by Woolworth's. While doing this, I happened to utter the words 'paper shears'. Her ivory brow smoothed out immediately. 'Oh,' she sighed, 'I can put down "Paper shears, five shillings". That's quite all right.'

I was delighted with this incident, but certain other features of the firm's economy were burdensome to me. The art department was supposed to 'pay its way'. Its share of the rent, light and heat of the building was added to my wages and the cost of art materials. This sum, I was warned, ought to be covered by the prices charged for the work although we all knew that these 'art' fees were frequently lowered until they were out of sight, to make the printing estimate acceptable. The layouts were really nothing but appetizers. This and other monetary equations I endeavoured to take seriously. I worked my brushes to the ferrule. As the other members of the staff clattered down the stairs in the evening, they called back over their shoulders, 'Are you staying all night?' The first person to arrive in the morning, finding me already there, asked, 'Have you been here all night?' I gave a mocking laugh, but I had. The solvency of the art department so worried me that I tried not to sharpen my pencils too often. Such flights into the absurd may have been launched partly by the trance of malnutrition in which I permanently floated. Friends prophesied that I would be blown away by the first winds of winter. I swayed obligingly but I did not grant their wish. I went on living.

I went on working.

The job meant a lot more to me than salvation from the fumblers' queue at the Labour Exchange. It hushed, even if it could not silence, the terrible things said about me by my relatives which, though I never heard them directly, reached me slightly blurred on the great family intercom. Also I felt that commercial art might become a permanent means of getting by. Being employed by the electrical engineers had only taught me how to ask where the gentlemen's lavatory was without blushing. Now I was learning something which might be really useful. I never thought of work as something that would one day earn me a lot of money. Squalor was my natural setting. I did not hope that a job would extend me to the limit of my talents. I hadn't any. What I wanted to wrest from regular employment was something with which to bargain with the heterosexual world for acceptance as a homosexual. This evangelical zeal was the real motive for everything I did. It would subside for a while and then flare up again – especially if my employer had recently called me into his office and made another attempt to coerce me into altering my appearance. Without looking at me and moving the papers on his desk from side to side, he would say, 'Fact of the matter is we don't particularly like employing people with plucked eyebrows and pointed fingernails.' For a week or two my eyebrows, which usually marched across my forehead in single file, were allowed to form fours and the style of my fingernails was changed from Gothic to Norman.

Surprisingly, I was not dismissed. On the contrary the day came when I was given an assistant. Thinking only of the havoc that an extra two pounds a week in wages would wreak on the firm's economy, I at first protested at this daring expansion. The directors, laughing heartily, pointed out how inconvenient it would be for them if, while I was the only member of the art department, I were to become ill or get run over by a bus. I asked them to provide me with a female assistant. I foresaw that there would be mutiny if a man were ever placed in a position where he had to do as I said. Whether my employers saw the sense of this I never knew but they pandered to my whim and engaged a charming girl with whom I worked happily for about a year. This was the first time I had ever been in the position of a master instead of a slave. I tried to behave with the utmost tact so as not to inflict on my assistant any of the humiliations that had been heaped on me. One day, however, presumably because of some special pressure of work, when she held a drawing up for my approval, I said, 'Yes. That's all right but the feet are bad.' No sooner had these harsh words passed my momentarily unguarded lips than I hastened to soften their directness with chivalrous obliquities. 'What I meant was', I began, 'that certain superficial critics might say . . .' At this point she cut me short. 'Thank God,' she sighed. 'You've said what you really mean at last.'

In all I was four years with this firm, earning for my last few months there three pounds a week. Then the business was sold and I sensed that, for all their courtesy, my new bosses were waiting for me to go. For the first time in a long while I took a look at the outside world. To my delight, I found that the storm had largely abated. Jobs were no longer hard to get.

Now they were only hard to keep.

Chapter Eleven

While I had not been watching, a number of tiny studios had sprung up at the tops of narrow buildings in Fleet Street and Chancery Lane. They had rather intimidating names like The Twentieth Century Advertising Service or The New London Studios. If I burst into any of these offices, I usually found two people playing table tennis in a nest of dirty teacups and the crumpled drawings of forgotten art students. One of the players would turn out to be the managing director and the other his staff. They didn't look pleased with my interruption of the day's business but now they would nearly always give me their attention for a few minutes, though this was frequently directed more at the art work I had done on my face than at anything in my book of specimens. When I had first come to London, I had seldom got as far as undoing the arm-splitting portfolio I then carried.

During the next two winters I worked in some of these studios, whose staff could hardly be seen with the naked eye. In the summer the tide of advertising always mysteriously receded, leaving all firms but those with the deepest roots high and dry. In this period of drought someone from all these smaller concerns had to be asked to leave. This was always me. My feelings on being dismissed were a mixture of indignation and relief. By the time I was twenty-eight, I had tired of this experience. I easily found a way of preventing its recurrence. I gave up work.

I became a free-lance commercial artist. I reached the Canaan of all the more optimistic art students of that time. Unlike modern students, none of those who were with me at Battersea Polytechnic ever thought of becoming a teacher. The girls gloomily guessed that they would go into lampshade factories and die there unless, before the red-sailed sampan or the pear with russet leaf got them, they managed to marry. They seemed to realize that this was a desperate choice. To St Paul marriage was barely preferable to hell. To women, though these two states may be the same, either was more to be desired than work. The male students tried to creep into studios or agencies, but only as a stepping-stone to those bright fields where they would work for themselves. From the very first week of their employment they started to collect printer's pulls of every brush stroke that they made – a tailpiece, a decorated initial. These they kept under their drawing-boards and fingered when the barrage of contemptuous criticism was loudest.

I cannot claim that from this moment I was always happy but, from the age of twenty-eight, I never did for long anything that I didn't want to do – except grow old.

I was elated by my freedom but I was anxious. Being a free-lance commercial artist would be taxing for anyone; for a person with no talent, it was hazardous.

I became a little man round the corner of advertising. I called on all the clients listed by all the studios I had ever worked in and offered to produce the same style of drawing as that to which they were accustomed, but more cheaply, more quickly and worse. This ruse worked admirably then. It would be of no avail now. During the course of my life-time, advertising has altered completely.

In that happy time when I first became a free-lance artist, advertising was a disgraceful trade. The confession that it was your chosen profession was received as though you had said, 'I'm in burglary.' It was run by businessmen who were presumed to have failed in more reputable concerns and staffed by artists and copywriters who felt that they were exiles from fine art and literature. Their function was to think up the atrocious pictorial and verbal puns, jokes and riddles (Sheila Dore drinking Oxo) that appeared on the hoardings. Then, at some time during the next few years, advertising became the great tax-evasion racket and everything began to change. Instead of nagging their agencies to do more for less, manufacturers began to implore them to think up ways of using up their vast 'appropriations'. Even I, who never worked in any large advertising concern, was later to attend a meeting at which a client said, 'But even if these counter-dispensers are invoiced at two pounds each and we foist one of them on every one of our concessionaires, that will only use up about two thousand pounds. We must get rid of twenty thousand before the beginning of April.' When this way of thinking became fashionable, advertising began to grow rich and attract an entirely different kind of employee – university graduates who brought with them a new ambience of fatuous elegance. If today you call on an up-to-date agency to hand in some copy for a two-inch single-column insertion in the daily press, you trudge through carpets as thick as pampas grass into a room lined with gilt mirrors. There a young man waits to extend towards you in perfunctory greeting at least four inches of cuff, transfiguration white. It is quite hard to remember that you have not come to have your hair waved.

In the 'sixties, if you told anyone that you were a practitioner of advertising, you would still be treated as though you had said you were in burglary, but morality had changed. The increased scale of your operations would lend you respectability. Who, except possibly the Postmaster General, would refuse to shake hands with one of the Great Train Robbers?

If, during my brief career as a commercial artist, any of these complexities were beginning to proliferate in advertising, they disturbed the atmosphere at a level far above my head. I merely ran in and out of business premises, studios and printers' works trying to persuade people to change their catalogue covers, posh up their letter headings or decorate their leaflets with catch-phrases or thumbnail sketches. My problems were small and mostly purely personal.

For anyone whose appearance is highly eccentric it is usually first meetings that are a special ordeal. In the days when I had looked for regular employment I had only the initial interview for each job to negotiate. Now that I was free-lancing, I had to face several such challenges every week. Since I depended for my livelihood on the goodwill of whomever I had come to see, these situations needed to be handled with much greater care than confrontations with strangers in the street. I found it necessary to develop a technique of being interviewed. This came into operation the moment I arrived at the reception desk. It began with not evincing any surprise as all the office boys fled through the doors nearest to them, firstly in order to fall about the corridors laughing without restraint and secondly so that they might spread to distant floors of the building the news of my advent. Then, while I waited for my appointment, I had to invent some artificial occupation for my attention so that it would seem natural for me not to look up as each member of the staff, carrying a meaningless piece of paper, came to speak to the receptionist. Finally there was the interview itself. At the start of this I must, by what actors call some piece of 'business', allow my client a good look at me while I was not looking at him. I did not always succeed in giving him time to put his eyes back in his head before I turned my gaze upon him.

Once the initial shock of seeing me had worn off, my interviewer was sometimes so relieved to find that I was not actually mad or even in any other way unconventional that he gave me work out of simple gratitude. A second visit was usually quite easy at top level though, by this time, all lesser personnel knew what to expect and the glass panels of whatever doors gave on to the route that I must travel were cloudy with the feverish breath of typists. It was now that I realized fully that, while I was apprehensive of strangers, any of the girls who might be forced to come close enough to me to hand me an envelope were trembling so that they could hardly stand. I never found anything except time that would remove this reaction of stark terror. In order at least to reduce it to a minimum, I cultivated an air of politeness bordering on subservience. Very slowly I was starting to go through that process that usually only convulses adolescents. I was learning not merely to confront people but to communicate with them.

In the outer world in which I was now struggling to make a living, prosperity was gradually returning to England. In the inner world in which I lived more intensely, things were getting worse. Possibly the two opposing trends were connected. It was only in the idealistic dreams of H. G. Wells that people became nicer as they acquired wealth. What in fact happened was that, as soon as men were released by affluence from the need for any unethical conduct themselves, they felt free to swoop down from their newly attained moral elevation upon the turpitude of others. To restore the self-esteem of which poverty had temporarily deprived them, the force of their condemnation exceeded the violence of any opprobrium that was formerly heaped upon them. In accordance with this rule, the fair name of vice was now being dragged through the mud by the English newspapers. It was hard to make dreary old fornication and adultery into news so the press directed the hostile gaze of the public towards the deviates. About the private lives of these more and more facts and pseudo-facts were coming to light every week. At first I imagined that this increase of knowledge would herald the dawn of a new day when the butch lion would lie down with the camp lamb. To my disappointment I now realized that to know all is not to forgive all. It is to despise everybody.

The first rumours about homosexuality that were now spread abroad brought only fear. They suggested that it was a much larger monster than had originally been suspected, devouring not only all ballet dancers and a few actors but thrusting one claw in at the front door of the homes of apparently quite ordinary citizens. The cry went up that England was going to the bitches. The police, to show that they took this prognostication seriously, began to clean up the West End.

Even when I had first discovered the Soho cafés certain older male prostitutes were taking their amber cigarette holders from their lips to declare that nothing was what it used to be – that the police had ruined Piccadilly; but in those days detectives chased me and my friends through the streets chiefly to satisfy their own hunting instincts. That their quarry was supposed to be a menace to civilization was incidental. They mentioned it only as, when blood sports are being denounced, huntsmen drag in the fact that foxes are a nuisance to farmers. We were not taken seriously. We were thought to be the exposed part of a very small iceberg. The general estimate of the number and kind of men who might be interested in us was even less realistic. One of the first policemen who ever questioned me at a street corner, when he had decided to stand a little closer and change his bullying tone to accents of fatherly concern, warned me that the only people who would go with boys were men suffering from venereal disease. They would be ashamed to communicate this to a woman. He may not have believed this story himself but he certainly expected me to.

Such naive ideas as this were now no longer in fashion. Police methods were growing very much grimmer. The decoy system became a nightly routine. Those of my friends who had previously dreaded that they might be hounded into jail now began to fear that they might be vamped into it.

The main field of operations for this particular strategy was the dimly lighted public lavatories in the less populous areas of London. While one detective in plain clothes wandered about with vigilant unconcern on the opposite side of the street, his accomplice, selected by his superiors because his natural endowments made him specially suited to the work, stood inside the urinal 'flashing' – demonstrating his do-it-yourself apparatus to anyone who happened to come in. (One cannot imagine how the kit inspection that would precede a stint of this duty would be conducted.) This trap worked well and by it many of the most unlikely people were lured to their doom. In modern times, when everyone knows about these manoeuvres, they are falling into desuetude. Common knowledge robs them of their effect. They also offend the sporting instinct of the British people. It is thought to be a dodge comparable with deliberately placing a diamond bracelet on the pavement and pouncing from ambush upon anyone who picks it up. Almost exclusively it ensnared borderline cases. Those whose idea of a lovely way to spend an evening was to wander from one 'gents' to another quickly learned to recognize a copper even by braille. It was persons who had never heard of homosexuality, but whose perfectly natural curiosity was aroused by any odd manifestation of human behaviour, who were in such danger from these police techniques. One can be sure that, even on a good night, merely to ask the constable what on earth he was doing would lead to an arrest; on a bad evening, a brief glance in his direction would be enough. But the worst result of the decoy system was that, in a policeman who did not happen to favour queers, being given the chore of making himself attractive to them rapidly turned his dislike into ferocious disgust. In return homosexuals who originally feared the police, which some would consider to be a good thing, came to despise them.

From the law's point of view the only weakness of the decoy system was that it took two constables to apprehend one sexual offender. This was a waste of manpower. The police thought of homosexuals as North American Indians thought of bison. They cast about for a way of exterminating them in herds. With the aid of informers they discovered where the great drag dances were being held and turned their attention thither.

These balls were organized by private individuals and held in any of the large banquet rooms that can be hired for parties. They couldn't, of course, be advertised, but no publicity was needed. The network always managed to reach any one who might want to go and had half-a-crown to spare for a ticket. About three-quarters of the men who attended these dances were in drag.

In a raid a hundred or more screaming, shrieking, fighting, kicking boys in feathered head-dresses and diamanté trains could be scooped, pushed or flung into vans by a relatively small squad of policemen.

Once, when I lived in Baron's Court, I travelled by

Underground to Piccadilly Circus wearing a black silk dress and some kind of velvet cape. I went to the Regent Palace Hotel, had a drink and talked airily of this and that with my escort, who was, I think, in a dinner jacket. Then I returned home. The evening was a triumph, in that it was boring; nothing happened. Since then I have never worn drag. Its only effect on me is to make me look less feminine. In women's clothes, even a faint Adam's apple, even slightly bony insteps are harshly conspicuous. I never attended one of these transvestite dances, but I very much doubt whether the charge brought against most of the guests – aiding and abetting an immoral performance – was founded on evidence. I suspect that they were very similar to the two or three drag parties that I have known. These were all exactly like one another. At none of them was there much sin. There was only a great deal of hysteria. I have sadly to say that to me everything about homosexuals was endearing except their gaiety. Being at a party at which they were having a really good time was like seeing a silent film of the 'twenties (with all the staccato haste and all the frantic mime) accompanied by a sound track recorded in the parrot house at the Zoo. I do not expect such parties are given any more. There is no need. Fancy dress has become national costume.

When these dances ceased to be given because they became too dangerous to be worth the pleasure, the police began to bend their ireful brows on the queer clubs.

To these no one in drag was ever knowingly admitted. An evening spent in one of them would almost always be quiet – even cosy. They were said to be places of assignation. They were to exactly the same extent as are all public houses, clubs and evening institutes. Who would go to a Morris-dancing class if the only hope were that it would lead to greater expertise in Morris dancing? Indeed is not the whole world a vast house of assignation of which the filing system has been lost? These clubs were merely places where men could talk, drink and dance together. It was the last pastime that so inflamed the imaginations of journalists but, though the foam dripped from their lips on to their typewriters as they worked, the word 'homosexual', by the constant use of which modern periodicals seek to make it known that they are serious-minded, was never written down for all the world to see. Even Lesbians, generally thought to be not so sinful because they were less illegal, were not mentioned in so few words.

Policeman: There were also present women – of a certain class.

Magistrate (rubs his hands): Prostitutes?

Policeman (in a lower voice): Of another class.

Magistrate (after a long indrawn breath): Oh! I see.

In spite of their tameness, all these clubs for homosexuals were raided sooner or later and the cases that followed enlivened the pages of the *News of the World* and the *People*.

The scandal of this kind that I remember best, because a commercial artist whom I knew was involved, concerned the Caravan Club. Proceedings lasted for a fortnight at the end of which my friend, though sentenced to two weeks' imprisonment, was released on the grounds that he had suffered enough in the police court. The proprietor, a certain Mr Neave, was clapped in for months. It is indicative of the over-simplified view of homosexuality that was still current that my friend took the trouble to persuade a young woman of his acquaintance to fluff out her hair and state in the witness box that she was his fiancée. This was supposed to make his visit to the club seem to have been a misguided sightseeing escapade. A present-day magistrate would merely think that the existence of the lady made matters worse.

I went to two or three of these clubs in my more optimistic days and observed that every year they grew more respectable or, at least, more restrained. Even in the beginning, when they were slightly sordid, I never felt at home. The management feared that my arrival and departure might draw the unwelcome attention of officials. This I understood but it was with pained bewilderment that I came to see that even among the clientèle my arrival caused a hush, clamorous with resentment.

I was beginning to meet a greater number and a greater variety of homosexuals and having to face the fact that, almost without exception, they did not like me.

Those who camped in private and watched their step in public felt that my not doing either was an indirectly expressed criticism of both these activities. They were right.

Though the strongest resist the temptation, all human beings who suffer from any deficiency, real or imagined, are under compulsion to draw attention to it. To their doing this I could hardly object since I was the living example of this obsession. But about camp, with its strong element of self-mockery, there seemed to me to be something undignified – even hypocritical. At its worst, it is a joke made by someone who acts in a certain way for laughs about a less fortunate person who makes the same gestures unconsciously. When I lived in Maida Vale in the flat of an invoice clerk, if I came into the kitchen and found him washing his socks, he could not have refrained from uttering some such phrase as 'A woman's work is never done.' I longed to cry out, 'You are washing your socks because they are dirty. The situation needs no comment.' I never did. I needed the room.

Even those who did not feel that I was secretly judging them were angry with me for presenting to the world, by whose good opinion they set great store, a brand image of homosexuality that was outrageously effeminate. This was resented chiefly by those who were effeminate but did not think of themselves as outrageous. Their objection was part of a much more widespread hostility to my putting forward any propaganda about the subject at all. Homosexuals generally did not look forward with pleasure to living in a world where the facts about their abnormality would be common knowledge and where even the least sophisticated people would learn to think of it as a possible explanation for any odd behaviour. An American actor expressed to me the view that obviously gay boys were 'spoiling it for the rest'. I was dumbfounded by this remark as to me 'it' was not a pitch but an illness. It was as though he had said that consumptives who coughed ruined for others all the fun of tuberculosis.

Publicity is annoying to some homosexuals because they enjoy living incognito. This allows them to practise a hoax upon society and particularly upon its women, with whom they carry on teasing flirtations. This masquerade seemed not merely unpleasant because it was contemptuous of the girls involved, but ultimately incomprehensible since the admiration or respect or love aroused were really for some other man of the same name. Possibly this perpetual confidence trick satisfied the hatred these men felt for the outer world.

One fact became inescapable. Homosexuals were ashamed. They resented not being in the mainstream of life. The feeling varied from irritation to the anguish of irrevocable exile. It had little to do with God or the neighbours or the police. It was private and irremediable.

Finding that homosexuals didn't like me was harder to bear than the hostility of normal people. To the latter reaction I had become accustomed long ago. There was even a sense in which I welcomed the animosity of the public. It seemed to demonstrate the necessity of my continuing to hammer away at them. The coldness with which I was received by my fellow-guests at small gatherings of the faithless was wounding in the extreme. I felt it amounted to ingratitude as I thought of my life as a burnt offering laid on the altar of their freedom. I could not see that this was but a contributory cause of their unfriendliness. If people speak badly of those who have done them a favour for which they have asked, what will be the attitude of those who find themselves in receipt of a sacrifice for which they have loudly proclaimed they have no use? This was a question that I never asked myself. I merely accepted an ostracism made complete by the fact that, owing to increasing police vigilance, the proprietors of even the wickedest cafés would no longer let me in. I looked increasingly for friendship among normal people. I put their tolerance to the utmost test not, as I imagined, by causing them to risk being involved in some wonderful scandal but by never talking for long about anything but the social problems of my kind.

Among those who now began to shoulder this burden was the wife of the unspellable Czech who had been brought to my room in Pimlico. She was an artist's model and dressed in accordance with the rigid dress laws of the time. She wore a vermilion polo-neck sweater, curtain-ring earrings and a black beret balanced at the ultimate degree of obliquity. Her days were spent working in the art schools and her evenings complaining of her husband who, in her absence, pawned her gramophone.

They were a lively pair, who lived in Warwick Avenue. To them I introduced my art school friend. At the week-end we often sat in the Czechs' basement flat talking of sex and eating a kind of sea-wrack produced by putting everything that guests brought into a huge saucepan that stood over the eternal flame of the studio stove. When no one brought anything, there remained the residual slime of past ages of prosperity. This we consumed with relish.

In this and many other ways Mrs Czech introduced into my life a new 'continental' flavour. I had no way of knowing (and no intention of trying to find out) if foreigners were really more lax than the English in sexual matters, so I had at least to affect to believe her when she told me that in Paris – and, she implied, in all the glittering capitals in Europe – homosexuals, so far from being objects of ridicule, were hardly noticed at all. She could not see why I did not either live flagrantly abroad or discreetly at home. She was sure the English would never abandon their condemnatory attitude towards me in particular and sex in general.

With all the other unfortunate people whom I had embroiled in endless screaming matches on this subject, there had at least been one point of agreement – that homosexuality was of the greatest importance. Mrs Czech merely thought of it as a minor, slightly curious fact of life. This disturbed my essential puritanism.

Every opportunity for pleasure that was offered to me automatically carried with it an almost equally strong desire to do without it. I might give way to either impulse, but the presence of the two contrary wishes was what gave zest to both.

In 1653, when God took a turn for the worse, the gusto with which the English took to a life of self-restraint undoubtedly contained an element of debauchery. If we don't suffer, how shall we know that we live?

One evening, while Mrs Czech was giving voice to her broad-minded views and I was shaking my thin-lipped head, I had interrupted her for a moment while I went to the kitchen for a cup. As I passed through to the other room of the flat, I came upon Mr Czech and the art student clasped in a passionate embrace. Here were forces of permissiveness that not even Mrs Czech would have condoned. But Mr Cromwell is not mocked. Soon the man in this sordid tableau was to go mad and the woman to become a nun.

I did not utter a word on seeing them nor did my feet falter but I was shaken by the revelation of two people, whom until now I had regarded only as reflections of my own existence, in violent relation to each other. For the first time I was forced to admit that other people existed. It was not a discovery that I welcomed.

Chapter Twelve

❧

During this period of my life – between the ages of twenty-four, when I started on what I imagined to be my career, and thirty, by which time I had abandoned this folly – my mother complained that my wanderings filled a whole address book, and her address books were not small. I did not have a restless temperament but I selected my lodgings on a fallacious principle. In my secret heart – or, to avoid exaggeration, in my secret space – I still thought of myself as living for others. My choice of a room was never dictated by taste or convenience. I gravitated only towards the greatest opportunity for putting myself at the mercy of other people and moved into a succession of places let to me by friends, and in some instances by mere acquaintances, who wished to lighten the burden of their rent but had no accommodation that they would have dared to offer to a stranger. When the discomfort and sometimes the downright degradation became too much for me, I moved on to fresh pits and pendulums new.

If I mention that I addressed even my closest friends as Mr This and Mrs That, it may be easy to guess how hard it would have been for me to reach any degree of intimacy with my own personality. I never called the various components of my character by their first names. Although it had been such a relief to live on my own in Denbigh Street, I changed my address eleven times before I finally gave up trying to disguise from myself my deep-seated indifference to the fate of others, settled into a room by myself and admitted that solitude was one of my essential needs.

The fact that I wanted to be alone did not mean that I disliked people. I liked my friends and I adored strangers. I have been accused of flirting with everybody, but my intention was not to arouse sexually. It was merely to entertain. Even a minimal remark about the rain provoked me to say, 'The weather's been nationalized.' If invited to the house of a friend, I was cosy, but should I find there people I had not met before, I plunged into a complete cabaret turn. I did not know that a reputation for wit is earned not by making jokes but by laughing at the pleasantries of others.

It was this mistaken idea that to win people I must dazzle them that made it essential for me to live alone. From time to time I had to stagger into my dressing-room.

I left my 6s. attic in Clerkenwell to share a room in Maida Vale with a disused actor. He slept in the only bed and I stayed awake bent like a jackknife on the sofa. After a while he started to bring strange men back with him in the middle of the night. In the morning, I frequently discovered that these were people who only a few nights previously had been trying to ravish me with one hand and rip off my wrist-watch with the other in Edgware Road. I was as embarrassed as Cardinal Wolsey at finding myself naked in the presence of my enemies. Also I had found my own sex life unpleasant enough. I had no intention of becoming a witness to anyone else's. I moved on to Lynhope Street where my stay was marked by only one incident. It was here that I was first visited by the police.

My Irish friend had disappeared some time back, but the Scotsman and the girl, who had finally come out in his favour, still kept in touch with me. My chief function in their lives was, when either of them was in jail, to keep them in touch with each other without the prison governor being apprised of any address but mine. This was how the police managed to establish a connection between them and me, and (probably when the young man failed to report to his probation officer) they called on me to ask for his address. I did not give it to them. I held the opinion that however low a man sinks he never reaches the level of the police. I and many of the thieves, prostitutes and other social outcasts who were my friends resorted to some very dodgy expedients in order to stay alive, but only the police habitually grovelled for their wages in the excrement of the world. The rest of us, however clumsily, however over-hastily, reached out towards life and love. Only the police trafficked exclusively in darkness and death. 'If you go on like this,' my visitor warned me, 'you will be charged with harbouring undesirables.' I pointed out that if my Scottish friend had been undesirable I might not have bothered. The interview came to an abrupt end.

Shortly after this I moved again.

At one moment I was sharing two rooms with the art student and at another I was the lodger of Mrs Czech.

Tired of taking off her clothes for so many for so little, she had become a nightclub hostess and required a lodger to help pay the expense of a WI address. This had to be someone who would not complain of the disturbance caused by her occasionally heaving semi-conscious men up the stairs in the middle of the night. For a life of this kind she was totally unsuited. She was not merely shy but innately respectable. It was therefore not long before she required yet another lodger. There were so few wolves at the door. I recommended that we should offer the last available room to the daughter of a clergyman whom my sister knew. This girl stole whatever money was left in the house, and finally revealed to Mrs Czech the secret that I had managed to keep for so long – that Mr Czech was living in open sin with the art student on Tower Hill. When questioned as to why she had done this, the clergyman's daughter said she was Mrs Czech's friend.

Against all odds, this story had a happy ending. Mrs Czech divorced her gramophone-pawning husband and married an habitué of the establishment where she worked. When they went to live in splendour outside London, my mother and I visited them and my lifelong admiration for men of action was increased a hundredfold. During our stay, I became aware of the terrible price they have to pay in their declining years. The new husband had been a born leader of men in some outpost of our not yet fallen empire. In retirement he found himself without inner resources of any kind. All the morning he wandered from room to room murmuring, 'When will we be having lunch, my love?' and throughout the afternoon he asked if it was tea-time. He did not partake of either meal, preferring to sit at the table sipping whisky while we ate. His inquiries were made only because he longed for some assurance that, though all else was now inert, time was still moving.

I had attended Mrs Czech's divorce breakfast but at her second wedding, which took place after a dignified interval, I was not present. I felt that this would not have befitted my station in life. By that time I had moved to Chelsea.

Here, in a mixed-with-water way, I lived the bedsitting-room existence, whose oddities Rodney Ackland used to flaunt before the amazed eyes of matinée audiences. I entered a boarding house as a foundation member almost before the paint on the backcloth was dry. It was run by actors and soon filled up with stock characters – an actress (tempestuous), a fashion artist (brittle), an American girl in search of experience (bewildered) – and we all ran in and out of each other's rooms making tea and talking about our futures. After a while this mixture was enriched by a touch of social realism. A coloured gentleman was added. The announcement of his arrival was made with a flourish to the inner circle as we sat in the basement awaiting our scrambled-egg supper.

Landlord: I want you all to know that there is a coal-black Negro living at the top of the house.

Lodger: Oh dear! And there's no lock on my door.

Landlord: In that case, Mrs Thomas, you will have to think of some other method of preventing his escape.

This was the first house I had ever lived in, including those of my childhood, which seemed to be home. As far as possible the outer world was excluded. Any real people who did succeed in crawling past the screening devices merely murmured to themselves, if they met me in the hall, 'That illusion again,' and went upstairs to take two aspirin. All the same I could not have said that I was part of a 'Chelsea' life. I knew only one bearded artist and only one model. I never went to a bohemian party and I never got drunk.

For about twenty years I lived in a state of intoxication with my own existence and, perhaps for that very reason, excess of alcohol was one of the extremes to which I felt no urge to fly. I asked many people why they drank so much but never received an explanation that I fully understood. It was the tales of their escapades while under the influence of drink that brought me nearest to comprehending their need for it. It seemed to give them a few hours of freedom from rules which, during the rest of their lives, they reluctantly obeyed. If this was true, then in the example of my life lay a cure for drunkenness, though it was hardly an answer which Harley Street would have approved. The prophylactic is, never to conform at all.

It was while I lived in Chelsea that I became a free-lance artist. Most of my nights were spent not in sinning but in executing the work that it had taken all day to wrest from the astonished fingers of manufacturers and publishers. When not busy in this way, if I went out at all, it was to visit friends.

One of these was Mr Cross whose life was a recipe for success. Never before and seldom since had I witnessed such indefatigability and such singleness of purpose. He wrote and he wrote and he wrote. 'I want', he exclaimed in an accent that you could have cut with a claymore, 'to have behind me a great body of worrrrrk.' He was twenty-two at the time. Even had I known that all this apparently fruitless effort would one day lead to his ruling the worlds of radio and television, I could not have followed his example. Industry of that intensity is composed only in part of energy. This I possessed. The rest is optimism, which I lacked.

Before my life became one long holiday, I was given a last vacation with pay. A few days of this I decided to spend in Portsmouth, which was in those days the Mecca of the homosexual world.

I could not do anything so brazen as openly to set out for the south coast in a spirit of hilarious research. Because the venture was motivated by sexual curiosity I had to arrange to be edged into it by quite innocent forces. I leaned forward so that fate could see me and waited. Soon an acceptable pretext fell into my lap.

The parson's daughter who had nearly wrecked my Czech friend's life was a student of drama (in so many ways) and through her I had already met a lot more embryonic actresses. They were kind enough to provide me with countless free seats for cultural plays from which I learned, if nothing else, that culture was not for me. Some years before I had given up reading. Now I was ready to give up theatre-going (unless it was free). I started to shed the monstrous aesthetic affectation of my youth so as to make room for the monstrous philistine postures of middle age, but it was still some years before I was bold enough to decline an invitation to *Hamlet* on the grounds that I already knew who won. Long after I had ceased to befriend the parson's daughter, I continued to see another drama student with whom she had once shared a room. This girl wanted to take a band of strolling – even meandering – players to the Isle of Wight to play Shakespeare's works in the open air. This scheme entered her head presumably because nature abhors a vacuum and also because every summer her mother ran a boarding house in Shanklin where she may have hoped her troupe could obtain food and lodging when all else failed. I was told about this project because my help was needed. The proposition was that I should lend her £10 and she would arrange for me to stay for a week free of charge in her mother's house.

I acquiesced in this on the grounds that the most anyone would expect from a holiday was a change of agony. It also enabled – nay, compelled – me to pass through Portsmouth.

Chapter Thirteen

❧

Like Florrie Forde, I and most of the homosexuals whom I knew best wanted 'something in a uniform'. Any national dress or occupational outfit may be sexually stimulating and there are as many kinks as there are kinds of costume. Uniforms appeal to devotees of the fearless man of action. They also pander to the Cophetua complex so prevalent among homosexuals. When any of my friends mentioned that he had met a 'divine' sailor he never meant an officer. Women seem to feel differently about these things. They prefer airmen, by which they always mean the higher ranks. I used to sit in the window seat in a King's Road café discussing these matters with a certain Mrs Gardner. Not long afterwards, she met Neville Heath. I should have guessed that she was a born murderee. She used to wear a leopardette coat.

When I was young the word 'soldier' meant one of the red-coated guardsmen who strutted up and down Knightsbridge in the evenings. These men were willing to go for 'a walk in the park' for as little as half-a-crown. This appeared to be what Berwick Street would call a desperate bargain at a never-again price but, had I accepted the offer, I have no doubt that I should have been beaten to a pulp with or without benefit of sex.

Sailors never asked for money but, on the contrary, had large sums of money to spend in short spasms of shore leave. They also never turned nasty. Perhaps the act of running away to sea was an abandonment of accepted convention and, after a sojourn in strange ports, they returned with their outlook and possibly their anus broadened.

The fabulous generosity in their natures was an irresistible lure – especially when combined with the tightness of their uniforms, whose crowning aphrodisiac feature was the fly-flap of their trousers. More than one of my friends has swayed about in ecstasy describing the pleasures of undoing this quaint sartorial device.

All that is ended now. Naval uniforms have been altered. With a vertical instead of horizontal opening to their trousers, sailors can walk their shoes to the uppers without a single stranger asking them for a light. They can linger even in Piccadilly without ever being offered a pint of beer. I was already long past the age when I knew or hoped to know any members of any of the forces before this happened, so I cannot say whether it was with a groan that the sea gave up its trousers. Among my friends there was certainly a day of mourning. As someone remarked, when told the new atom bombs would explode without a bang, 'They can't leave anything alone.'

Today a visit to Portsmouth would not be worth the train fare, but in the summer of 1937 the whole town was like a vast carnival with, as its main attraction, a continuous performance of H.M.S. *Pinafore*. As most of the men were in uniform and the girls wore shorts and bras in the street, it seemed that everyone was in fancy dress. This much I saw from the taxi window while I was being driven towards the hotel which the driver had chosen. 'It'll be the best – for *you*,' he said. He may simply have meant that it was one where I stood a good chance of being let in. Having been refused admittance to many restaurants and even a few cinemas, I had wondered whether I would meet with any trouble of this kind, but none occurred. With a poker face I thanked the young man who carried my luggage upstairs for both pieces of information when he explained where the gentlemen's and a moment later where the ladies' lavatories were.

When I had unpacked it was about six o'clock in the evening. I decided to lie down for about half an hour to rally my forces. I overdid the relaxing rituals and fell asleep. I got up the instant that I awoke but, by the time I had clapped on as much make-up as the forces of gravity would allow, it was night.

Outside the hotel I paused for a second, not knowing which way to go. A second was long enough. I was instantly surrounded by sailors. I explained that I wished to walk along the seafront and they offered to show me the way. From then on our progress was like a production number in a Hollywood musical. The chorus was continually on the increase as my guides called out to their friends who, even if they had been going in the opposite direction, turned back to join us. When we arrived at the seafront as many of us as could sat on one of the seats while others perched on the railings. The beach was strewn with lovers, and even a few couples sleeping with their children and their luggage beside them. The distinction between indoors and outdoors, which in England is usually so marked, was temporarily suspended in a hot gauzy trance.

The sailors told me how to recognize the north star and explained various quaint items of nautical lore. I expressed suitable amazement, addressing my remarks to the sea. I quickly found that if I spoke directly to any one of my companions he blushed and the others hit him till he fell off the seat. There was a great deal of laughing and flopping about, but the conversation never fell below the level of the risqué. There were no threats, no insults – and very little personal interrogation. The only question I remember being asked was one that was always cropping up in those days, 'Do you know Fred Barnes?' A few years later this became 'Did you ever meet Fred Barnes?' for he had committed suicide.

After a while, when it became obvious that there was going to be speech but no action, without becoming angry the sailors began two by two to drift away until I was left with two castaways – older men who had once been in the navy or possibly merely wished they had. These walked back with me to the hotel, which turned out to be shut. I was surprised, having imagined in my Monte Carlo dream that all seaside hotels were open all night. To my companions this was one last huge joke. They took me to a place where we would be able to sit around until daybreak. This too was shut. My escorts banged on the doors until, with a rattling of chains and a creaking of hinges as though we were about to enter a dungeon, we were admitted to a huge canteen full of down-and-outs. The proprietor had hair so red that the pigmentation had flowed out into every visible inch of his skin and even into the pinks of his eyes, as the colour of flowering cherry trees stains their leaves.

The place we entered was just like the dining-hall at school except that there was a large tea urn on a counter that ran along one end of the room. We ate as much as we could, to make it worth the redskin's while to have undone all those bolts. Then we settled down to innumerable cups of tea. Our chatter and our laughter awoke other inmates. They lifted their heads out of their plates and crossed the room to join us in yet more rounds of teas. When I judged that it must be daylight in the streets, I crept back to my hotel. I had been speaking off and on (but chiefly on) for about eight hours. I slept until the following evening.

I never saw Portsmouth by day.

When, the morning after that, I sat in the early train back

101

to London, I tried to recall what adventure, what romance I had expected this visit to offer me but, as though I had seen the movie after reading the book, reality had now obscured the dream. I had beheld a miracle. That was the first, last and only time that I ever sat in a crowd of people whose attention I really desired without once feeling that I was in danger.

For this reason all the quality of that evening, and all the evenings like it that never came, remained with me for many years until I no longer felt the need for this kind of relationship with this kind of person – until my desires had changed and my whole nature had coarsened in a way that on that night in Portsmouth I would have thought impossible.

Chapter Fourteen

❧

At that period of my life the average length of my tenancy of any one room was about four months, so I would have described myself as having lived in Chelsea for a long time. I was there just over a year. Towards the end of my stay it transpired that I had only imagined that I was among friends. When I had already given notice, I was accused by one of my landlords of stealing money from the room of another tenant. After a day or two the lost purse was found but no apology was offered. I was then accused of having put it back. Of the two indictments the latter was by far the more annoying. I have never had much respect for the law, including the law of property (though, until St Genet set his famous example, I had never thought of boasting about this), but I was very indignant that my enemies should suddenly pretend to think me likely to give way to remorse. They had constantly exclaimed that I was ruthless. This last epithet, although it was intended as an insult, I had always covertly regarded as praise. Gestures of atonement sickened me. Unless it was by accident that I caused harm to somebody, I never apologized. Pardon, sought or granted, was to me a fatuous social flourish. It was a further infliction of cruelty on a victim, forcing upon him who already had some ill to bear the humiliating chore of uttering a few words of feigned forgiveness.

I no longer inhaled a permanent atmosphere of dis-approval but suspicion, once aroused, automatically fell on me. (I do not think that, to this day, things have changed much in this respect.) Also it was only when I was already leaving that people's true feelings emerged in the same way that, in the street, the whistles and the cat-calls began not when I was approaching but when I had already passed by.

I took up residence in a mews in Belgravia as the lodger of a teacher of ballet. She had rented a huge barn of a place with a view to sleeping in it by night and giving lessons there by day.

Living in this mews placed us at the bottom of a deep ravine formed by the five-storey houses of the rich. From the top back windows of these mansions, the last members of the dying race of domestic servants looked down – but not in mercy. When I first moved into my room I had no curtains and later, when these were provided, I seldom drew them. This was a difficult operation necessitating a climb on to my desk since even the bottoms of the windows were above my head. What could be seen of my room was the bed. On this there was usually somebody lying. Since there was only one chair in the room – an upright wooden one that I used when sitting at my drawing-board – there was nowhere else for my friends to relax. I soon received my second visit from the police. This time there were two of them – a detective-inspector and a younger man with no speaking part who merely stood by the door as though he half expected he'd have to prevent me rushing hatless into the street. The inspector explained that he had called because of complaints lodged by the neighbours that they could see into my room. What they saw they didn't like. It is said that when Mae West was told that Americans complained of the suggestiveness of her radio programme, she drawled, 'They could've turned it off.' My sentiments were the same, but my aplomb was not. With downcast eyes and scarlet cheeks, I promised that in future I would be careful what I did. This seemed to be an insufficient answer, for the policeman then shouted, 'Things go on in this house for which the penalty is seven years' imprisonment.' This was the first time that the laws regarding private indecency had ever been brandished before me. I remained calm and a few minutes later he left. As he did so he told me his name twice, as though, if I ever decided to give myself up, he expected me to send for him. As soon as my visitors had left, I telephoned all those friends who might not wish to call at an establishment that was being watched by the police. I started with a man, fairly highly placed in one of the ministries, with whom, after many years of happy celibacy, I was having a dismal affair. His terror of disgrace was such that he never visited me in daylight. He was careful to telephone a few minutes before his arrival to make sure that no one – not even the ballet teacher – was on the premises.

All liaisons between homosexuals are conducted as though they were between a chorus girl and a bishop. In some cases both parties think they are bishops. I realized I was a chorus girl and quite happily knew men for as long as seventeen years without knowing their surnames or their addresses. Anyone who allowed himself to become my friend was doing me a favour. I always tried to make it clear that I was aware of at least some of the penalties that went with knowing me. Before a relationship had gone very far, I usually explained that, in difficult circumstances, I did not expect to be acknowledged. I only ever knew one woman who did not treat this remark as an attempt to put the loyalty of my friends to the utmost test. One day, as I was walking wickedly up Rathbone Place, I saw her coming innocently down accompanied by an anti-hooligan whom I guessed to be a client of the firm for which she worked. Talking airily in millions she passed within a foot of me without either of us glancing in the direction of the other. Neither of us mentioned the incident subsequently but, from that moment onward, with that woman I felt absolutely free.

There were others, however, whose very fear seemed to urge them to defy the world. Once I was invited to the house of a movie writer with the words, 'Mrs Smith will be here with her two children. She comes from Pinner. I can't imagine what she'll make of you but still . . .' When I remarked that it would surely be better if I came on a different day, my suggestion was swept aside as though I was being morbidly sensitive. At the great confrontation, as I stretched out to this woman a hand weighed down with coral and turquoise, my host said to her, 'You can touch him. He's quite real.' Until that moment, she had been doing all right. She had doubtless thought, 'I'll ask my husband about this when I get home' and then made her mind a complete blank. As soon as the remark about me was uttered, she was visibly stricken with embarrassment. So was I. At one time Crisp's First Law would have stated that those who most fear disgrace invariably behave outlandishly. Now I see that I mistook the cause for the effect. It is those who, for some unknown reason, have no idea how they will behave in a social emergency who quite naturally dread the world's censure.

On this principle the man from the ministry continued to visit me and, on one occasion when I was clambering about on the furniture, said that he couldn't think why I bothered to draw the curtains. I took no notice of this foolhardiness. As it happened, the threats of the police never came to anything. I was not arrested for many years and, when I was, the circumstances were different.

While I lived in Belgravia, two new ways of supplementing my fitful income from commercial art presented themselves. The first of these was writing, at which so far I had never had the least success. The Blandford Press, for whom I had often designed a book jacket or laid out an advertisement in one of their magazines, suggested that I should write a book about window dressing. I had never thought of doing this because I knew nothing about the subject. The publishers did not think that this was any handicap, so I flung myself upon the project with all my half-starved weight and quickly wrote thirty thousand words. I had only one idea to put forward – that, in any visual field, maximum interest lies at the point of maximum contrast. After several shaky years the book sold its edition. This only proves once more that people will pay to read what they already know. I made £60 but, though I have written one book and a few articles since, I cannot say that my hope that writing might become a second career was ever fulfilled.

The other profession in at the door of which I desperately thrust my lacquered toe was tap-dancing. My landlady did not want pupils who wished to learn other forms of dancing than ballet to be turned away for lack of a fully equipped staff of experts. This was another subject of which I was totally ignorant, though this weakness never came to light. Only one student with tap-dancing in mind ever turned up and she was a beginner. I taught her by keeping one tap ahead at each lesson. The occupants of the workshop below had to endure a noise overhead like an African hailstorm beating on a tin roof while I hastily practised what I had just been taught before my pupil arrived to learn it. The steps were not made any easier for either of us by the clearly audible curses from below. To those poor workmen peace only came with the outbreak of war.

When war was declared I went out and bought two pounds of henna.

Chapter Fifteen

❧

If any astrologers have read this far, they will now wave their star-tipped wands over their heads and jump up and down with glee until their pointed hats fall askew on their silvery locks. I was born under Capricorn and am logical to the point of idiocy. Having learned with such difficulty to go about the streets amid cat-calls, raspberries and flying stones as though nothing unpleasant had happened, I decided to make use of this capacity for feigned indifference and treat all signs of hostility with contempt, even now that they had transcended the personal and were on a national scale. Apart from getting in a good supply of cosmetics, I made up my mind to ignore the war as completely as I could.

I never bought newspapers, for fear that people might think that I liked what went on in the world, and I had long ago given up listening to the radio the moment that I realized that it was always going to be jolly without ever being witty. Therefore the news of Hitler's move into Poland was brought to me by a new Irishman who often called on me to beg for half-crowns, which I liked, and to bring me in exchange stolen silver spoons, which I loathed. While he was still with me the air was filled with a fluctuating wailing sound. 'What's that?' I asked. 'Oh, they're just trying something out,' my friend replied. Thus the first air-raid warning came and went.

One thing the war compelled me to do was to change my address twice more in a frantic search for cheaper and ever cheaper rooms. All work had ceased for me. The money that I had in hand dwindled fast. But, though I now sank socially from Belgravia to Fulham and later Chelsea, there was a sense in which these moves were for the better. The ballet teacher had virtually given me the furniture that she had bought for my room while I was her lodger. This was a stroke of wonderful good fortune. I would never have been able to spare at one time enough money to furnish a room and I totally lacked the resources of character to arrange for delivery to my home. A great many transactions that involved dealing with strangers were still quite beyond me. Though I had progressed far enough to be able to hail a taxi or even ask a policeman the way, I could not have acquired a passport or opened a bank account. Now, without having to make a fool of myself in any specific way, I had come quite effortlessly by the means to take unfurnished rooms. I took two in rapid succession. The great space famine had not then begun. I was able to look at several possible premises in a single afternoon. The second move I made more or less at random but the place suited me so perfectly that I have lived there ever since. I had thought once before that I had reached home. Now I really had.

The unfurnished life was different from the furnished in many ways, all of which were improvements. Now for the first time I had life on my own terms. I decided immediately that I would never become a thrall to rituals of domesticity.

In my childhood I had seen these engulf half my mother's life. Sitting on the floor watching her take from a bookcase and dust every single one of the works of Bulwer Lytton, I said, 'I shouldn't do all that.' She replied, 'I know you wouldn't. That's why I must.'

Perhaps because of such memories as this, squalor rapidly became my natural setting. I felt it was only by a series of unfortunate accidents that till now I had always lived in the captivity of hygiene. Nancy Spain had not yet become one of the sages of the air and had therefore not had the opportunity to promulgate her first law – only a fool would make the bed every day – but this was one of the truths that I knew by instinct. As soon as I began the unfurnished life, I practised sleeping on my back as still as if I were in my coffin. I slid out of bed in the morning like a letter from an envelope. Except for the thickening film of sullied cold cream that as time went by piled up on the pillow-slip, no one would have been able to detect that my bed had been occupied. I changed the bed linen once a week. I realized that if I did not, I would one day reach a point of no return beyond which the laundry would refuse to accept my dim grey sheets. This Augustinian state of affairs was acceptable when I slept alone but it would no longer do once I was not sure that this would always be so. About cleaning the rest of the room I did nothing at all. Except that after a while it became necessary to jump in the air while putting on my trousers so as to avoid trailing them in the dust, I never found that this omission brought in its filthy wake any disadvantages whatsoever. As the years went whizzing by, I was able to formulate a companion law to Miss Spain's. Mine stated that there was no need to do any housework at all. After the first four years the dirt doesn't get any worse. Later, on the Third Programme, I was given a chance to deliver this message of hope to a drudging world.

After an absence of fifteen years, Mr O'Connor, once a hooligan like the rest of us, stood on my doorstep. He wanted me to take part in a programme about eccentrics. Ever delicate in these matters, I asked, 'What's in it for me?' He assured me that I would be paid and ran back into the street to bring in a 'tape' machine. Holding a microphone in front of my face, he said, 'Say something about life and death.' As I break out into a cold, quicksilver sweat at the mention of one and elevenpence I was amazed to receive later a substantial sum for sitting in my room and talking about myself. If only I could get some of the back pay!

I doubt if my words were heard by many inveterate dusters and sweepers or if the conventual rigours of Woman's Hour were subsequently relaxed, but we must not mourn. The measure of a woman's distaste for any part of her life lies not in the loudness of her lamentations (these are only an attempt to buy a martyr's crown at a reduced price) but in her persistent pursuit of that occupation of which she never ceases to complain. Although housewives know deep down that they are doing, if not what they like, at least what they prefer, this does not prevent them from envying the tousled bliss of others. In tones of asperity, the ballet teacher once said to me, 'No wonder you have the time and energy to be nice to everybody. You never do any housework.'

When I had lived in my room for some fifteen years, and I was feeding a starving outcast, we were called on by a small deputation of guests from a party going on elsewhere in the house. They brought glasses of sherry. As the rest of us sipped and chatted, one visitor sat silent. Through thick horn-rimmed spectacles he gave the scene a panoramic stare. His name was Mr Pinter. Later he confessed that this was the moment when he first felt that he might write a play.

To the unfurnished life I found I could add a whole new dimension by installing a telephone. This gave me people to nod to not merely up and down King's Road but ranged hundreds deep into the uttermost distance. Even when I had returned to my room defeated by not finding any of my friends in their homes, I could still by telephone pan the suburbs for a few last nuggets of conviviality. This instrument was like a window which gave not only on to the world I knew but also on to one full of strangers.

Through it work came to me from publishers I didn't know and bookings at schools I had never heard of. I turned it on as other people switch on the radio. The programmes were far more interesting. A pessimist is someone who, if he is in the bath, will not get out to answer the telephone. I was incorrigibly hopeful. I never willingly let the telephone bell ring for fear that I might miss a message from God. The first words I spoke into the receiver used to be 'Yes, Lord.'

After a while, if you have a telephone of your own and billing in the book, you have appointments with fear. Most of mine were merely tedious – an extension of the treatment I received in the street. Strangers, refusing to give their names, claimed in would-be sexy voices to know me intimately. They sometimes rang me more than once in an hour. Presumably they hoped to make an appointment that they would not keep at some windy street corner miles away. Others only wanted to amuse their friends. These could be heard giggling at the other end of the line. After many years these calls thinned out, but they never ceased altogether. It is hard to imagine what pleasure can be gained from listening to a tired voice repeating over and over again, 'What is your name and what do you want?'

Remembering my own disappointment at learning that there was no confederacy among homosexuals, I felt I must try wherever possible to come to the aid of the party. If one of these telephone conversations began with a white-faced voice saying, 'I must see you,' I always invited whoever was speaking to visit me. I chose a time when I would be at home whether they arrived or not, in case this too was a hoax. I realized that I was placing myself in some danger. Before the stranger was due to appear, I put on my shoes (which I almost never wore indoors), locked my money in a cupboard, put the key in another cupboard and locked that. Then I was as ready as I could be although there was still a vulnerable moment when I opened the front door. There might be a whole army of ill-wishers on the other side of it. There never was. Indeed most of the people who visited me in these circumstances seemed more apprehensive than I. One looked as though he would not get up the stairs without a blood-transfusion.

As soon as I had led him into my room, I offered him a seat and said gently, 'Now. What's your trouble?'

Stranger (almost in a whisper): There's no trouble.

Me: Then why are you here?

Stranger (becoming agitated): I don't know.

Me: You mean you came here for no reason at all.

Stranger (the words bursting from his pallid lips like a cry of anguish): They dared me to!

I rose to my feet and he to his. In all he had only been in the room about three minutes. As I accompanied him down the stairs, I said, 'I don't advise you to treat any other eccentric old gentlemen in this way. They might be even more annoyed than I am.'

Chapter Sixteen

❧

As the meteoric dust fell invincibly and insatiably on the early Caledonian Market furnishings of my room, I sat and waited for my call-up. Although I now had no work to do it was not hard to fill in the time. While other districts of the trembling city were busy fire-watching, learning first aid and digging incomprehensible trenches in London squares, Chelsea was occupied exclusively with amateur theatricals. Wearing steel helmets and gas-masks, air-raid precautionists and auxiliary firemen hastened along King's Road. If asked by anxious civilians what was up they said in tense voices that the pantomime rehearsal had been changed to half past six at the Town Hall. Apart from shows arranged with a jolly laugh by absolute amateurs there were also innumerable productions put on quite seriously by semi-professional actors in dim billiard halls in Notting Hill Gate.

Through a Miss Murison, who later knit her soul more permanently with the theatre by marrying Paul Holt, I became connected with one of these ventures. She asked me to write a revue. When I had finished it, I found the idea had been abandoned some time back by her co-directors in favour of a production of *The Scarlet Pimpernel*. As the stage of the theatre at which this play was put on was the size of a kitchen table (but not so strongly constructed), the great whirl of the ballroom scene was difficult to manage. Indeed the whole play suffered from its constricted setting. An exiled aristocrat entered through a doorway so narrow that she was compelled to hold down the wide brim of her hat against her ears. When first seen she appeared to be wearing a poke bonnet. A moment later, when she let go of her hat brim, she seemed to have on her head a great flapping bird that was finding it difficult to settle on a moving perch.

This ill-advised production was followed by a work called *Fishing for Shadows*. Acts two and three were still being translated while the first part was already in rehearsal. Miss Murison had asked the young man, a Russian, who was doing the play from French into English, for a comedy to 'take people's minds off the horrors of war'. She had received his word that this was just what *Fishing for Shadows* would do. Almost every page that he handed her contained another suicide. At length Miss Murison felt compelled to seek reassurance by asking, 'You did say it was to be a comedy, didn't you?' The young man indignantly replied, 'It's as funny as *The Seagull*.' Now that his reputation has reached its full scale we can assume, which no one dared to do at the time, that this was a joke. The translator's name was Peter Ustinov.

Except in the incompetence of their productions neither of these shows was typical of the output of the little theatres of that time, all of which had a more or less homogeneous policy. Before the rise of Joan Littlewood there was a great gulf fixed between the commercial theatre and those far-out playhouses that presumptuously described themselves as non-profit-making. They meant 'loss-making'. There were always more people on the stage than in the auditorium. The West End managements provided patrons with a glimpse of wickedness that never sank lower than adultery sketched in with a kiss before French windows. In Notting Hill Gate producers went in for works whose style can best be described as Venetian kitchen sink. In these the

115

rape, murder and incest that were one day to become more a part of family entertainment than scenery or footlights stalked the stage clothed – nay, swaddled – in verse more blank than even John Dryden would have dared to write. Some of these poetic dramas went so far that not even highbrow audiences could swallow them. A young man, so dedicated to one of these theatres that he painted the scenery by day and acted in front of it in the evening, described his agonies as he tried to think of some way to prevent the house from bursting into unsuitable mirth at his first line. This was 'The Pope's gone mad.'

Feeling, as it turned out wrongly, that my innate theatricality must one day pay off, I tried my utmost to attach myself to one of these theatres. After my abortive revue, I wrote an anti-Pirandello play so bad that to this day I cannot see why it was never staged. I also witnessed with conscientious regularity the plays of my friends. Such entertainment as I was able to extort from these visits to the theatre came from sitting in the bar drinking a little and talking a lot. Once, I was thus engaged at the Chanticleer with Peter Noble, who in those days was already a well-known writer of theatrical gossip, and also an actor. A woman darted out of the auditorium to hiss at us, 'We can't hear a word in there.' 'Then prop the door open,' said Mr Noble.

A letter requiring my appearance before a medical board reached me in the first April of the war. This was early, for I was already, in fact, thirty years old, but when, some time back, people had called at the mews to ask impertinent questions about my sex and age, I had stated that I was twenty-five. I had not done this because I was eager to denounce a monstrous tyranny but to bring nearer the moment when the problem of how to avoid starvation would be taken out of my hands. Many of my friends were able to find work in camouflage. This seemed an unlikely way for me to earn a living. My function in life was rather to render what was already clear blindingly conspicuous. In spite of the frantic efforts I had made in so many directions to fortify myself against destitution, in a national emergency it transpired that I was utterly useless. It was almost enthusiastically that I set out for the drill hall in the middle of Kingston to which I had been summoned.

I was fully prepared to march at the head of my men, an occupation in which I had had considerable practice, but the authorities were not having any of that. The moment I stood naked before the first doctor, Harley Street collapsed. I was surprised. My appearance was at half-mast. I wore no make-up and my hair was hardly more than hooligan length. Many of my friends on seeing me thus would have cried out, 'Whatever's happened to you?' but of course my hair was still crimson from having been persistently hennaed for seven years and, though my eyebrows were no longer in Indian file, it was obvious that they had been habitually plucked. These and other manifestations of effeminacy disturbed the board deeply. Even while I was merely having my eyes tested, I was told, 'You've dyed your hair. This is a sign of sexual perversion. Do you know what those words mean?' I replied that I did and that I was homosexual. The doctor who had asked the question immediately left me to whisper to one of his accomplices. Within a minute the entire governing body had gone into a spasm of consternation behind a hessian screen leaving the would-be members of the forces to shiver in their nakedness and urinate into an assortment of bottles. After a while a great effort was made by everyone to regain composure and I was passed on to another doctor. He asked me why I had dyed my hair. While I was filling my lungs with air in preparation for delivering one of my favourite speeches of self-justification he shrugged his shoulders and said, 'I suppose you prefer it red.' Having expected some brand of Hippocratic remoteness from my examiners, I could hardly conceal my amazement at their awful humanity. It was as though a chemist were to wink at a customer buying a French letter.

From my hair, interest passed to my anus with which two of the doctors tampered for some time. Their private dreams of what the lives of homosexuals were like must have been very lurid. When I was vertical once more, one of them asked me if I thought I could walk four miles. I, who had stalked the streets for hours, was secretly piqued by this but from lifelong habit I forbore to show my irritation. I said I thought I could but it was obvious that no amount of humility would now avail. The tide of opinion had turned against me. When I had been sitting alone in another part of the hessian forest for a few minutes, a young man appeared holding at arm's length, as though he were about to read a proclamation, a sheaf of papers which he tore up with a flourish. 'You'll never be wanted,' he said and thrust at me a smaller piece of paper. This described me as being incapable of being graded in grades A, B, etc. because I suffered from sexual perversion. When the story of my disgrace became one of the contemporary fables of Chelsea, a certain Miss Marshall said, 'I don't much care for the expression "suffering from". Shouldn't it be "glorying in"?'

I was totally exempt.

My ministry friend had warned me that I would never be called up. As he had had experience of the First World War, I should have believed him. I had laughed him to scorn. I had assumed that the authorities would realize that, without my hair, the mandarin half of my fingernails and a few other detachable adornments, I would pass in the gun smoke

118

for an ordinary mortal. I was wrong and had now been given the most bottomless sack of all. I thought of myself as deprived by prejudice of a glorious and convenient death. I had absolutely no visible means of support.

With a slightly annoying air of spirituality many people have expressed in my hearing the opinion that financial worries, however grave, were never the worst of their troubles. Certainly the two people whom I nagged into describing their nervous breakdowns never mentioned poverty even as a subsidiary reason for their collapse. They named two main causes. One of these was God, from whose territory I had withdrawn my ambassadors at the age of fifteen. It had become obvious that he was never going to do a thing I said. The other problem was love – a word about whose meaning there seemed to be some ambiguity.

Often during this period of my life, to the embarrassment of my hearers, I claimed that my whole existence was love. I meant that I was trying never to close my hand against anyone – even the unlovable (in dealing with whom I was having a great deal of practice). I would have placed at anyone's disposal my meagre resources of money or advice or concern. Sometimes I fancied that all the elements of a golden age of universal well-wishing were already known and would become instantly effective when, as with the components of D.D.T., some genius combined them in their right order. I was always delighted with the slightest break-through in this field.

There was a restaurant that I frequented because it was so small that by speaking slightly above normal pitch I could fuse the private conversations being carried on at each table into a general discussion. Here, an elderly lady seated at the table nearest to mine nodded her head discreetly in the direction of my soup and said to her companion, 'That looks nice. I wonder what it is.' I took a spoon

119

from one of the unoccupied places at my table, dipped it into my bowl and held it to her lips. For a doubting second she telegraphed a helpless glance to her friend and moved her hand to take the spoon from me. Then she leaned forward and, like a child, tasted the soup while I held the spoon. 'It's very nice,' she said. 'We'll have some.'

The only thing at that moment that could have brought the golden age nearer would have been if I had been able to make her drink from the spoon I had used.

The idea of love as a universal accessibility was not merely different from other people's. It had nothing to do with it. The consuming desire of most human beings is deliberately to plant their entire life in the hands of some other person. For this purpose they frequently choose someone who doesn't even want the beastly thing. I would describe this method of searching for happiness as immature. 'Immaturity' is one more word that requires definition. To men it means the inability to stand on one's own two feet. A woman flings it at anyone who doesn't want to marry her. Here I find myself for once inclined towards the masculine view. I feel that, though no one must ever deny his dependence on others, development of character consists solely in moving towards self-sufficiency.

In adolescence I searched diligently – even dangerously – for some sheet-music kind of love that would fulfil the erotic dreams the literature read to me in my childhood had coloured so romantically. In this fantasy I would be the cherished object of some great man's total preoccupation. In return I would become his perfumed slave. Of course I was willing to adopt this attitude of abject prostration only before someone who never asked me to do anything I didn't like. As soon as a man demanded that I modify my scandalous appearance or agree to being passed off as someone's nephew, my love, which was a chronic invalid, died in an instant.

This idea of love I abandoned in my twenties for something which I thought nobler, though really I was merely throwing over Elinor Glyn for Patience Strong.

At one time I imagined my sexual abnormality constituted the whole of my difference from other people; later I decided that the rift was caused by my exalted views on love. Finally I saw that these two causes were interdependent. Universal love goes with masturbation.

In an incorrigible fantasist, auto-eroticism soon ceases to be what it is for most people – an admitted substitute for sexual intercourse. It is sexual intercourse that becomes a substitute – and a poor one – for masturbation. If this is evil then Baden-Powell, instead of urging the male adolescents of the world to take colder and colder baths and make wilder and wilder assumptions about the stuffiness of their mothers' views on puberty, should have found some way of warning boy scouts that alienation was the probable result of this habit. I regard this alienated state as good. It grants the intellect some freedom from the body. It saves a person from judging others by the confused standards of male, female, old, young, beautiful, hideous, in a way that can never be achieved by eating vegetables or sitting cross-legged in the middle of California or wearing purple on Wednesdays.

This was the state of mind at which I had now arrived. Though I treated even the slightest variation in my relationships with other people as a fascinating crossword puzzle, the problems that arose were not aggravated by sexual frustration. They caused me concern but not anguish.

I had severed the connection between sex and love. It wasn't the complete solution to the human predicament but it was a help. It enabled me to make the contrary statement to that made by most of my friends. My only serious problems were financial.

The trouble with this state of blessedness was that when money difficulties arose, they seemed total. I did not live simply in order to be solvent, but as soon as I was not there was nothing in my life that made the ensuing hardships worth bearing.

When a third wave of poverty overwhelmed me, I knew with even greater certitude than when I had lived in Clerkenwell that the only complete solution to my problem was suicide. I never brought it off. I was afraid. A lifetime of never making positive decisions, accepting instead the least of the evils presented to me, had atrophied my will. It was not so much that I longed for death as that I didn't long for life. Emptiness, though, was not a sufficiently definite feeling to lead to a violent act. Instead of sitting in my room and balancing the relative convenience of various ways of ending it all, I ought to have been busy trying to summon up a reasonable amount of despair. Hopelessness was thinly spread like drizzle over my whole outlook. But, in an emergency, I could not find a puddle of despondency deep enough to drown in.

Chapter Seventeen

❦

For several weeks after my rejection by the medical board I lived on borrowed money and, without warning them, crawled round to the houses of my friends at meal times. Getting back into a commercial studio turned out to be impossible. Whenever I applied for a job I was careful to explain that I was totally exempt but I was always obliquely accused of being a pacifist. Even when I protested that I was one of the few people who actually liked the war, I still didn't get taken on.

The only money that I can remember earning at this time came from Mr Hall. Without ever having met me, he telephoned me to ask if I would allow him to paint my portrait. When I asked if he would be willing to pay me he said with frankness, 'Only if it's absolutely necessary.' It was.

The moment that he opened the door of his studio to me, I recognized him as one of the landmarks of the district. I had often witnessed him in King's Road wearing a huge black hat and a stiff pointed beard with which it would have been possible to scrub the sink. He was the first real artist that I had ever met. I was delighted that he looked so perfectly the part. His home was also the first studio that I had ever entered. I exclude those bedsitting-rooms which are so sparsely furnished and so lavishly unkempt that their occupants feel the only thing to do is call them studios.

My friends – even those that lived in Chelsea – received

the news that Mr Hall was painting me (and might do a picture of me in the nude) with amused contempt mixed here and there with a sickening archness. Some openly suggested that he had proposed this out of sexual curiosity. Even in those days, long before Mary Quant and John Stevens turned the place into a vast boutique for the rich, Chelsea was evidently not, as advertised, the home of the broad-minded. It was merely lousy with people who lacked the nerve or the energy to give positive expression to moral judgment. Indeed, if a bohemian is someone without prejudices and without roots, then what there was of the *vie de bohème* seemed to reside in Mr Hall.

I was flattered by his interest in me and charmed by his courtesy. He utterly lacked the brutish iconoclasm with which many seek to establish themselves as 'characters'. His melancholy dignity, however, baffled me. I sometimes thought he would have liked to shed this but couldn't. He answered with candour even such questions as 'Why do you paint?' but I never got to know him.

And I tried.

I tried hard, for I wanted to enter the world of which I felt he was a consul, though I knew that I would be an impostor there. I don't hold with art.

The only time I gave a gracious nod in the direction of culture was when surrealism came to London. This movement appealed to me because the pictures executed under its banner were akin to the works to which my mother had directed my attention in childhood. Their especial quality was Victorianism now put into a perverse form. I was only sorry that this was not enhanced by giving the paintings such titles as 'The Blight of the World' or 'When did you last rape your father?'

In spite of this minor disappointment I went to the famous exhibition in the Burlington Galleries where I found myself an unwitting, though not entirely unwilling, exhibit. In and out of the different rooms glided a certain Mrs Legge wearing full evening dress and carrying in her hand an uncooked pork chop. With orange face and vermilion lips I weaved my way past her, clanking with amulets, but, as her face was entirely covered by a hood of roses, I could not see whether she registered fear that I might be a materialization of the surreal world or annoyance that another voluntary worker had got his rota mixed with hers. For a moment one of the dearest wishes of surrealism was fulfilled. The barriers between art and life fell down.

Subsequently cultural trends soon restored and even reinforced them. I came out on the side of reality. I began to feel that art was not merely superfluous but actually insulting to life. Its implication was that the visible world was intolerable unless a bunch of amateurs at the creation business shoved it around. For this reason I never wanted to paint but hoped, to borrow a phrase from the jargon of a later aesthetic movement, that I might become an *objet trouvé* in the world of art. Some of this hostility to culture I may have expressed when talking to Mr Hall. If I did, it may have formed a part of the barrier between us.

I got to know slightly better a writer who occasionally came and sat with us while Mr Hall worked at my portrait. I attended a small party at this man's house. One of the guests, who managed to wear his naval uniform as though it were really only fancy dress, sang himself to bits. He shouted, shuddered, hooted until the sweat poured down his face and his hair fell into his eyes. Among the young, such behaviour is now as common as smoking reefers, but at that time it was a startling phenomenon. I enjoyed his performance a little less for fearing that he might have a stroke. I need not have worried. Soon he was carrying on like this several times a night. It was Mr Melly. He had a genius for getting others to see a joke as he saw it and this won my admiration but, whenever we met in later years, my part in our conversations consisted chiefly in saying 'Sh-sh'. Mr Melly had to be obscene to be believed.

In all, Mr Hall painted three portraits of me. The fees he paid me for sitting for these were very helpful, but I had the misfortune to outlive them. I reached the end of my tether and the tethers of most of my friends. I was rescued by the documentary movie industry.

Chapter Eighteen

∾

I seemed always to be walking along a corridor flanked by doors barred against all knocking, all entreaty. These were interspersed with other doors looking exactly similar but which opened almost before I reached them. I now came to one of these.

While I had been living the furnished life in Chelsea, among the inmates of the house in which I lodged had been the secretary of a film producer. As well as she could she had explained me to her employer. Without seeing one of the dingy letterheads and layouts of advertisements in such papers as the *Fur Times* and the *Cactus Journal* which were pasted into my book of specimens, he had offered me the job of lettering the titles of a number of travelogues he had made in pinkest Petra and other cities of the Near East.

All but one of these had been distributed before the war started. The remaining one was now brought forward by another producer who, when my work for him was finished, distributed me among the poor of the documentary industry. I could hardly keep pace with the work, partly because there was so much of it and partly because the lettering of a film was never commissioned until a few days before the trade show. The movie business has a genius for bringing some kind of chaos out of order.

Of course lettering credits was only another form of commercial art. It required the speed, the high gloss that I had always lacked, but because it was connected with the movies, for me it had glamour. I flailed my limbs so wildly in my efforts to cling on that at one moment I caught hold, by accident, of an art directorship.

I had been called by telephone to the top floor of the building over a Chinese restaurant in Wardour Street. When I arrived I was asked by a man with a delicatessen accent if I would paint the sets of a film that was to go into production there the next day. I had never painted scenery in my life, but I said I would if he would tell me what I was to do. When I turned up the following day, this man was not present though a great many other people were. None of these seemed to know anyone else or to have the faintest idea what he himself had been hired for. I wandered round the room eavesdropping at various uneasy conversations as though I had gate-crashed a dull party, until I arrived in a corner where one man was asking another, 'Well, what's it supposed to look like?' Then he had an idea. 'Let's ask that bloke with the funny . . . Oh, here you are,' he said as he caught sight of me. Explaining me to the other man, he added, 'He's your art director.'

'Oh, am I?' I squeaked, delighted but surprised.

With the swiftness of a tropical sunset assurance faded from the faces of both men. My moment of glory had come and gone.

Working for the movies was the first job I ever wanted to do for reasons other than to show I could. For once, though I was prepared to accept defeat, I did not intend to embrace it. I wanted to be what would now be described as the Saul Bass of British movies and, to this end, I abandoned for a moment my existentialist posture. I applied for and, to my amazement, obtained a job in Studio Film Laboratories. This was a mistake. I was not able to flit from room to room learning the secret of the celluloid universe. I was confined to the art department where, even if my ineptitude had not almost immediately been unmasked, I do not think I would have lasted long. My presence caused agony to the head of the studio. From lifelong habit I called him 'Sir', never noticing that every time I did so he winced. Also, after a few weeks, he became aware that other members of his staff had learned by heart and were starting to use the detestable curlicues with which my discourse was decorated – nay, cluttered – and which later came to be called Crisperanto.

Within nine months I had once again been given the sack. All that I had succeeded in doing was to go out of circulation for long enough for most of my movie connections to forget about me.

Life was a funny thing that happened to me on the way to the grave. I had never thought of my progress – perhaps we had better say my movement – through time as a triumphal march, but at this point I felt that I had stumbled. It is only when looking at an aerial shot taken by memory that I see how little was lost by my failure in the movie industry. If I have any talent at all, it is not for doing but for being. In the humblest way, this I was now given the opportunity to demonstrate.

I became a model.

Chapter Nineteen

❧

In my final week at Studio Film Laboratories, I received a telephone call from the model I had known when I lived in Chelsea the first time round. She implored me to go and pose in Toynbee Hall in her stead. This was not as far-fetched an idea as it may sound. The sending of substitutes to art schools is as common among models as the parallel practice is among orchestral musicians.

'I've telephoned everyone,' she said. 'They're all booked.' Then she added in a voice that carried a faint tone of bitterness, 'You're always saying it must be nice to be a model. Now's your chance.'

As soon as I had put down the telephone receiver, I flew at one of my older pairs of underpants and – with those very same paper shears that had once nearly brought disgrace upon me – cut away everything but the waistband and a small triangle of fabric in front. I had been an art student and knew that in England (though not, I was told, in Germany or any of the Scandinavian countries) male models were never quite naked before a class containing female pupils.

The following evening I arrived in Toynbee Hall for a four-hour evening class. I was eager but a little apprehensive lest I should faint as I had often seen models do. As I stepped on to the 'throne', the master said, 'I suppose you couldn't hold on to the top of that screen behind you in a kind of crucifixion pose?' I pointed out that I had died after three hours last time. This idea was abandoned, but I was asked to stand for the whole lesson (with the usual ten-minute breaks every hour). I was glad of this. It made the evening a representative test of my endurance. When at ten o'clock I found myself still conscious, I knew that yet another way of earning a living had been presented to me.

Though being a model was such a great physical strain, there was a sense in which the work was easy to do. It required no aptitude, no education, no references and no previous experience. You had only to say 'I do' and you were stuck with it like marriage. It was also easy work to get. The war was on and I was almost the only roughly male person left with two arms and two legs. I applied to the Secretaries of many of the London schools and a few of these gave me work, but it was the suburban and even provincial schools that kept me busy. To these I was recommended first by other models, who were amazingly kind to me, and after a while by the instructors. In a frantic effort to be full-time part-time teachers and so earn colossal temporary wages for forty or more hours a week, they rushed from one county to another snatching up in each the maximum number of hours that the Ministry of Education would allow. Once they discovered I was reliable they took me with them – frequently by car. One of the worst hazards of teaching 'life' was the lack of dependability in models. Nowadays big schools employ 'battery' models. Their engagement lasts a whole term or even a year. In those days bookings were often given six months in advance and the work was 'free-range'. It was spread over the term in odd patterns – six Mondays, perhaps, for portrait or every Wednesday of the term for sculpture, depending on the school's curriculum. By the time these scattered dates came round the person engaged

131

for them had often found elsewhere a full-time job that he preferred. There were only a few devotees of the profession. Even in those days someone masquerading as a model was frequently only a typist with romantic ideas, a hooligan in need of funds or a dancer who hadn't made the grade. In the suburbs, the non-arrival of the model was a disaster. A replacement could not possibly arrive until the middle of the day and by then the students, always on the boil, would have wrecked the place.

Posing was the first job I had ever had in which I understood what I was doing. Always until now I had worked or tried to work to a standard other than my own. In commercial art I had always made an effort to draw things so that others would find them appetizing and worth their money. Even in my book I had attempted to describe ideas so that others would find them interesting. For some artists and writers this may not be difficult. They may have tastes they share with the average consumer or the gentle reader. I had so little in common with real people that someone once said to me, 'I think I like things better before you've praised them.' In these circumstances it was hardly surprising that my drawings and my writings brought me so little success. I decided to set about the job of modelling in the opposite way – to force upon the students the qualities that I felt life drawing ought to possess.

When I had attended the art school in High Wycombe twelve long dark years before, the hours I had most enjoyed were those spent in the 'life' room but, though some of the models had been of a beauty like the sun, hardly any of them had seemed to me to be doing enough. They had stood or sat or lain about like ordinary mortals and not a bit like the figures of Michelangelo. I wanted to change all that. I was an avowed enemy of culture but I admired his work unconditionally.

Of all the paintings from the nude that I ever saw, only his appeared to me to be not merely of living people but of what it is like to be alive. The drawings of Ingres, continually held before the lustreless eyes of students as an example for them to follow, always seemed to me to be seen from outside – to display a lascivious preoccupation with surfaces – with the convexities and concavities of the body. Michelangelo worked from within. He described not the delights of touching or seeing a man but the excitement of being Man. Every stroke he made spoke of the pleasure of exerting, restraining and putting to the utmost use the divine gravity-resisting machine. His work had the opposite quality to the paintings of Rembrandt, into whose canvases the subjects stumble, broken, conscious of their physical faults and begging the beholder for forgiveness.

I was determined to be as Sistine as hell. It was fully in accord with my endeavour to live in the continuous present from head to foot. Unfortunately I was not naturally equipped to carry out this mission. I was undersized in all respects except for a pigeon chest and a huge head. When stripped, I looked less like 'Il David' than a plucked chicken that died of myxomatosis. It could hardly have been otherwise. I had lived most of my life by starving and gorging alternately and had never taken any exercise other than walking the streets. However, I twisted and turned, climbed up the walls of life rooms and rolled on their paint-daubed floors morning, nude and night for several days a week for six years.

The students were furious.

I had not foreseen this. I had only anticipated hostility from the staff, thinking of teachers as thin, bespectacled, Gothic creatures hysterically concerned for the reputations of their schools. This turned out to be a false image. Art masters were at great pains to distinguish themselves from

133

other pedagogues. Even in those days they were deliberately jolly. When, with time, even teachers of academic subjects began to relax their forbidding posture, art masters found themselves compelled to resort to a rusticity amounting in some cases to oafishness.

Even those who were embarrassed by my antics remained kind. Unhooking me from the picture-rail, they would say quietly, 'All you have to do is to stand as though you were waiting for a bus.' What kind of an injunction was that when, at a bus stop, I looked as though I were on the dais of some life room? One man, working on the Sickert principle, went so far as to assemble a washstand, a cracked basin and a dim grey towel in the hope of toning me down. As I stepped in among these negligently posed props I asked, 'And how do you propose to make me look like home?' The instructor who had gone to all this trouble breathed deeply down his nose. 'There you have me,' he said.

Aware of this difficulty most teachers simply turned me loose on the class. As I stood *en arabesque* on top of a pillar, Mr McCullough said, 'Now draw that. Wings optional.' He was secretly filled with a fiendish glee at seeing his pupils struggle with a subject that not even they could take for granted. My poses were so extreme they could not be held long enough to suit a painting session. I worked chiefly in drawing classes. I preferred them. Drawing is a science; painting is just something for the long winter evenings.

More than anything it was the fact that my contortions made their work more difficult that caused the students to manifest such hostility. When I had first seen the boys in their corduroy trousers and the girls in their Hungarian blouses, I had assumed that I would get on all right with them. It had been many years since I had been in a crowd of young people. I had forgotten or had never really known what they were like.

The young always have the same problem – how to rebel and conform at the same time. They have now solved this by defying their elders and copying one another. The result to grown-ups is that they seem brutish and stuffy at the same time. The fact that I was eccentric did not prejudice them in my favour. I was peculiar in a manner other than theirs and my naive enthusiasm merely highlighted the fact that I was a generation older than they. I was a senile delinquent: in their eyes an unforgivable sin.

Towards the end of the war art students became very numerous. Perhaps drawing was a pleasant distraction from the bombs before which some people tended to go to pieces. When peace broke out, their number did not decrease. The Minister of Education ran down to the water's edge and, as our brave boys disembarked, scattered grants to art schools over their heads like confetti. Some fell on men whose art training had been interrupted by their service with His Majesty's Forces; some reached stockbrokers, stevedores, street-walkers and stage-managers. Everyone who could availed himself of the Minister's kindness. The chance to study anything without paying fees, even if it is something that can never be the slightest use, must not be allowed to pass by. In this way the Great Art Rush began. Gone were the dignified days when an intending pupil visited the principal by appointment and was advised which classes to attend. Now, on the first day of each session, a mob of would-be students pressed with Klondike intensity against the entrance to every art school in the country waving their grants above their heads like prospecting claims. At ten o'clock, when the doors opened, the crowds surged up the stairs and sat down wherever they could. If, by some miscalculation, anyone found himself in the lavatory, that was what he studied for that term.

The climate of art was milder than it is now. The

enmity felt for me by students remained for the most part unexpressed. I was part-time sacred – a hated demi-god who occasionally became an object of reverence. Once in a while a female student, to show her peers that she could, would make bringing me a cup of tea a pretext for sitting on the corner of the throne and talking.

This sometimes led to trouble.

There are girls who do not like real life. When they hear the harsh belches of its engines approaching along the straight road that leads from childhood, through adolescence to adultery, they dart into a side turning. When they take their hands away from their eyes, they find themselves in the gallery of the ballet. There they sit for many years feeding their imaginations on those fitful glimpses of a dancer's hand or foot which seats in the upper parts of theatres afford. When I was young I too 'adored' the ballet. For me its charm was that one of the dancers might break his neck, but what appeals to these girls is the moonlit atmosphere of love and death which the withering hand of truth can never compromise. During the intervals they hold hands, numbed by excessive applause, with the homosexual young man who is bound to be sitting on their right or left. Even the boys, who have no positive intention of deceiving them, are drawn into a relationship damaging to the girls. After a lot of squeaking at the bus stop when the ballet is over, the young men pursue on the way home other interests, which at least yield a morsel of satisfaction. The girls can do nothing but return to their joss-stick-perfumed nunneries. From this position there is no way back. They can only stay where they are until, in middle age, they awaken to the realization that they don't know a single person who isn't queer. Then they move on to the uncharted quicksands of nudism, Yoga, vegetarianism and other diseases of the soul too terrible to name.

Some of these girls are innocent enough to think that these unreal friendships will lead to true love – a kind of sexual intercourse that will happen to them without their having to take too horribly much notice. Even those who are sufficiently sophisticated to know that this will not be so persist in these relationships. They provide an opportunity to lavish emotion upon a pseudo-man without paying the price that in heterosexual circumstances would be inevitable.

Apart from the young woman who threw herself on the linoleum of my room in Denbigh Street, I met several other girls of this kind. One overtook me in Smith Street in Chelsea and begged me to teach her to paint cats; another wrote me anonymous poetry in care of a café where I used incessantly to sit. The worst case that I ever had to deal with occurred shortly after I became a model.

The day before one Easter holiday, I was standing in the corridor of a vast technical college outside London waiting for my wages. A student with whom I had exchanged a few polite words came up to me to say goodbye. It was her last day. I was still trying to think of something eternal to say when she suddenly seized my hand and kissed it. The moment I had recovered from the shock, I glanced up and down the passage to see if there had been any witnesses to this blurring of my public image. Then I turned to ask the girl what on earth she thought she was doing. She was already running away, as well she might. I later realized that her behaviour was the result of having read a book by Mrs Nijinsky, in which she describes a similar gambit in her merciless pursuit of her husband. On finding this partially reasonable explanation of the event, I regained my polar calm. A week or two later the girl wrote to me asking if we could meet. Foolishly thinking that all I represented to her was a glimpse of the life beautiful,

I suggested that, after a Sunday morning class at her old school, I should bring her back with me to London, give her lunch in a hooligans' restaurant and take her to tea with someone sufficiently untidy to pass for a genius. This scheme was put into action, and all seemed to be going well until we were standing in Holborn amid the usual crowd of hostile witnesses waiting for a bus that would take her home. Then, without even a cry of warning, she flung herself upon me with a weight fit to bring me to the ground and implored me to kiss her. I was very annoyed. Straightening my knees with a great effort I said sternly, 'You had better catch your bus.' This she did, but the hideous entanglement did not end there. I received a letter from one of her friends entreating me to continue to see the girl. The implication was that suicide would follow if I refused. I replied explaining that I was homosexual and that, as we now all knew that a beautiful friendship was not all that was expected of me, further meetings would be a complete waste of time. It took several other letters saying the same things more and more unkindly to bring the relationship to an end.

A friend in the forces to whom I described by post this chain of degrading incidents replied, 'How could you have been taken in by all that soul-mate rubbish?' My sin had not really been naivety but vanity. I had, as always, been reluctant to forgo a single ounce of friendship and had imagined that, by strength of will and the use of an unremittingly antiseptic manner, I could have and hold the situation on my own terms.

Another friend who was told the tale asked me what the girl looked like. When I described her, he said, 'But if she had been good-looking and as masculine as you are feminine (if such a thing were possible), would not her advances have been acceptable?' By asking this question he showed me that to him and doubtless to many other people, an effeminate homosexual was simply someone who liked sex but could not face the burdens, responsibilities and decisions that might crush him if he married a woman. This idea seemed to me totally erroneous. It left out altogether the devouring preoccupation with the male sexual organ which, as soon as his erotic habits are completely formed, becomes the main and finally the only interest in a homosexual's life. The question was put to me quite sincerely by an entirely heterosexual man. This showed me that in normal love the emphasis was not on the sexual organs. The relationship was a clash or a union of personalities laid bare by sexual passion. Between two men it consists of each using the utmost force of his personality to gain access to the sexual organs of the other. Of this situation I was not yet in my own life aware.

Chapter Twenty

❧

Most of the models I knew I had met very casually while we stood in some secretary's office or waited in the tea queue of a school canteen. We flexed the muscles of our bare feet and pooled the misery of our falling arches and distended veins. There was one whom I met by formal introduction. Just as I was about to begin work in one of the top floor rooms of St Martin's School, Mr Hofbauer came and stood at the foot of the throne. He was really the art editor of Ivor Nicholson & Watson, but occasionally he disguised himself as an evening student. He told me that the man posing in the next room wanted to meet me. I went next door where, not in entire forgetfulness but in utter nakedness, this other model and I bowed and shook hands.

When the class was over he suggested that we should visit one or two of the cafés which he frequented in Charlotte Street. If it had not been for this casual invitation, a whole world might for ever have remained closed to me. By night, when these places came most vividly to life, no one who had not a pathfinder's badge could have reached them. The black-out made them indistinguishable from the ordinary shops on their right and left. Even if I had known their whereabouts, I would never have dared to enter them alone. Eating under the ferocious scrutiny of strangers gave me indigestion. But once I had been introduced by an habitué and found that my appearance was acceptable there, my whole social life changed.

Until now my evenings had been spent lying down (to recover from the strain of standing for seven hours) or writing to my mother or mending my socks or having a good cry. Suddenly all these activities, which I had regarded as mildly pleasant before, were brutally squeezed into hidden corners of my leisure so that I could devote two or three nights a week to sitting in one or other of the cafés in Charlotte Street. This occupation represented far more than a change of pastime; it marked the discovery of a new self. To go with my public face I now began to construct a public character. I moved from concentrating on individuals to dealing with crowds; but with a difference. In youth my object had been to reform. I now wanted to entertain. Here the reformation had already taken place. I was moving among people to whom my homosexuality was of no consequence whatsoever. I began a whirlwind courtship of an entire district.

In appearance these cafés were just like those from which I had been barred fifteen years before in Old Compton Street. In all other respects they were very different. Many homosexuals were present but there was no element of camp. They were also quite unlike the places which were to spring up fifteen years later where, amid the excruciating discomfort of industrial design and the cacophony of guitarists, people of all ages could be seen teenaging like mad. They even differed from their contemporary counterparts in Chelsea, which were clean to the point of primness and riddled with an artiness which I now saw to be but a feeble pretence of bohemianism.

In Charlotte Street there was a sound of revelry by night and London's capital had gathered then her beauty and her chivalry and bright the lamps shone on brave women and fair men. There was a marvellous generosity about the way the restaurants were run. The helpings were large, even

141

discounting the portions of drowned cockroaches which were served, at no extra cost, with every dish. The staff was friendly and unhurried to the verge of immobility. So was the clientèle: bookies and burglars, actresses and artisans, poets and prostitutes; and there was an entirely new caste brought into being by the war – deserters. These did not merely frequent the cafés. They couldn't leave. In a smoky cellar called 'The Low Dive' they stayed for weeks at a time. Ultimately this place was closed by the police. This seemed a foolish move since the deserters there could be taken in the swarm. With this subsection of hooligans I had a special bond, because I had two exemption papers. One had been flung at me by the medical board and said that I suffered from sexual perversion. Another sent to me by the Labour Exchange presumably out of sheer kindness gave no particular reason for my inability to enter the forces. These I could lend to anyone who wished for a few hours to leave his hide-out. It was only necessary for the deserter in question to decide whether he preferred the hardships of jail to the disgrace of being Quentin Crisp.

Despite the variety of classes, sexes, nationalities and callings represented in the cafés of Charlotte Street, there prevailed an effortless acceptance of the other person's identity. There were rows – even fights – but I never heard any cattiness. I was never told any scandal.

From my point of view it was the restaurateurs whose broadmindedness was most amazing. Whereas in Chelsea eating-houses I was on sufferance and was warned not to sit near the window, in Charlotte Street I was not merely accepted without question but was frequently given meals on credit. Occasionally I was even lent money by the proprietor to buy black market goods that the customers and the staff were perpetually offering for sale.

The only people I ever saw turned out were those who

combined fighting too much with eating too little. Even for these exile was never intended to be permanent. When Toni tired of a rowdy group of girls he flicked their bare arms with a wet tea towel. They left without taking offence to return later, with cheerful grins and long sleeves.

I still sometimes dabbled in commercial art – usually by doing book jackets. These were the commissions I liked best. They did not necessitate doing a drawing so large that distant parts of it could only be reached by pinning it on the wall (I never owned an easel). On the other hand none of the work was so small that it could only be done with the aid of a magnifying glass. Also the amount of lettering involved was seldom great. I learned to handle books so that they fell open at the murder and, even when this did not happen, I was soon able to read through them rather than read them. The narrative evaded me but the style in which it was written told me what kind of reader it was intended for. Once I knew this, designing the cover became simple. If my eye was caught by the words, 'Her eyes filled with tears and her bosom rose and fell,' it was obvious the book was meant for women (pastel shades, dark-haired heroine with shallow cleavage); if the novel had been written for men it would have said, 'Her huge breasts shuddered with emotion in their strait-jacket of pink satin.' (Dark tones, red-haired heroine with deep cleavage.) If in three hundred pages there was no mention of breasts at all, the volume must be a documentary (no illustration) or for children (bright colours, mouse-haired heroine with *no* cleavage).

These rules applied at that time because the intentions of publishers towards readers were still honourable. Now that the marketing of all goods, including books, has become a shameless hoax practised on innocent consumers, the works of M. Zola are packaged to look as though they were by

Mr Spillane. This ruse works because no one would dare to take a book back to a shop because it wasn't as filthy as the cover promised.

Among the firms for whom I most often worked was Messrs Ivor Nicholson & Watson whose art editor told me that if I wanted to write something for publication, the time and place were now and here. During the war, though there was a widely advertised paper shortage, publishers would issue any old muck. Even so I thought it prudent not to attempt anything long. I decided to write a mere pamphlet in verse. The idea for this had come to me some time before when a friend had uttered in my hearing a limerick about a Kangaroo who offered himself to the Zoo. It ended:

> But whenever he tried
> The committee replied,
> 'We already have plenty of you.'

But the time I next saw my friend I had added a second verse:

> If you like you may leave us your name
> So that we may go into your claim
> And then doubtless you'll hear,
> In the course of the year,
> An evasive reply to the same.

My friend said that this had now become a slashing indictment of the Ministry of Labour. I rather shakily agreed but, even when elaborated into forty-eight rather clumsy verses of angerless satire, the idea seemed to need something else to make it worth a publisher's while. I decided to try to ensnare Mr Peake into illustrating it. He was at that time the most fashionable illustrator in

England. In spite of this he frequently sat in the Bar-B-Q in Chelsea and was not in the least inaccessible. When talking to him I allowed it to seem that Messrs Ivor Nicholson & Watson had already commissioned the book and he declared himself willing to illustrate anything that was certain of appearing in print. These words had hardly issued from his lips when I leapt up and ran all the way to Manchester Square to tell the publishers that Mr Peake was simply dying to illustrate a book I had written. They expressed their interest in anything that Mr Peake chose to work upon. Running to and fro and making a series of statements that seemed increasingly positive but could never be used against me was much harder work than writing the verses. These only took two afternoons. That was as it should be. It was certainly not the writing but the chicanery that ensured publication.

When the book came out, anxious to know if sales were booming, I crept into Hatchards where a pile of copies was on display. To my delight there was a man staring at the uppermost of these. This, however, turned out to be Mr Peake.

I do not think *All This and Bevin Too* can have been a triumph. Although I was immediately commissioned to write (and paid for) another book, the second was never published.

I sank back into oblivion.

I saw myself sinking and would have cried out for help had there been at hand anyone who could have been the slightest use. Coming closely upon my defeat at the hands of the movie industry, this failure to reach the literary big time might have been hard to bear had not my social life at that time been so eventful.

Chapter Twenty-one

❧

Into the Cuzco of the layabout civilization came a man who
was the size of a barn door and as easily pushed to and fro.
The night I first saw him he was badly in want of a meal
but, as soon as some supper was placed in front of him,
his great shock of white hair fell forward on to the mound
of chips on his plate. More than food, he longed for sleep.
I took him home with me. Nothing reared its ugly head.
The man slept and slept. The next morning when he was
leaving, I nodded towards a small bundle of possessions
that he had brought with him and said, 'You can leave
your things there while you're looking for a room.'

Three long dark years later they were still there.

At first our association consisted of my meeting him in
Toni's or The Scala. To both of these I went at least twice
a week. I brought him back to my room if he needed a
good night's sleep. Heaven knew where he kipped when
he was not with me. After a while, he formed the habit of
visiting me every week-end and my life became a series of
Saturdays for which I prepared and Sundays from which I
recovered, but I never gave up hope. I never let more than
a few hours pass without including in the conversation the
words, 'When you have a room of your own . . .' and I
never gave him a latchkey. I knew that once I had done
that I was a lifer. In all other respects my manner was, as
one of my friends said, 'dedicated'. Because I could tell that
he had never known a world in which he had the upper

hand, I became his slave. When, presumably to normalize our relationship, he suggested a little sex, I concurred. A year or so later, in the middle of a sketchy embrace, he said, 'Let's pack this in.' I said, 'Let's.'

Like the heroine of *The Garden of Allah*, I put my love to the utmost test.

It failed.

Shortly before one Easter holiday I told him that it was time I visited my mother for at least a week-end. These words touched his sensibilities. He was deeply devoted to his mother. He gathered up his things and left. As he did so he said, 'I don't see what I've done wrong even now.'

He had done nothing wrong. He could do none. He was a man without guile. His only fault was that he existed. His parting words would have reproached me till my dying day were it not for the fact that, immediately after the war, I heard that he was married. This was an outcome of which I had despaired. I knew he was Kinsey-queer rather than coot-queer. He merely associated with homosexuals because they bought their love by the pound. He had gravitated towards Charlotte Street because there people were so appallingly equal. I had feared he might never marry because his idea of courtship seemed to be a few neolithic lurches towards the object of his desire. Living with him was the practical part of an examination in the theoretical section of which I had already done badly. In the second half I scored no marks at all.

Having lain alone for thirty odd years I found that I could not fully relax if I shared my bed with anybody, let alone someone of Barn Door's dimensions. Never get into a narrow double bed with a wide single man. After a while we took it in turns to sleep among the dust on the floor and wake in the morning more or less flock-finished. The routine of my life was altered in areas which I had thought

147

were fixed for all time. We ate at home on Saturday and Sunday evenings. I was compelled to shop – an activity which I had gradually reduced to a minimum so as to avoid the veiled insults which, together with inferior goods, were heaped upon me by salesmen.

In the matter of clothes I was supported entirely by voluntary contributions, like a hospital, and, when introduced to anyone, however interested in other parts of their bodies I might be, I always looked first at their feet to see if these were as small as mine. I hoped their cast-off footwear might be given to me. The trouble with shoes is that they are unalterable. All other clothing I accepted indiscriminately. I could at any time enlist the services of a certain Mrs Markham, known throughout Soho as the greatest trouser-taperer in the world.

Thus the need to visit men's-wear shops had been almost totally eliminated, but no way had yet come to hand of acquiring second-hand food. I was compelled to buy it new.

If in the future a doctor discovers that certain diseases are indigenous to homosexuality, one of these will be a distended bladder – the result of trying to avoid the risk of arrest automatically incurred by using a public lavatory. The other will be vitamin C deficiency acquired because the staff of vegetable shops are so impertinent that one would suffer almost anything rather than deal with them.

Having put up with Saturday morning's round of humiliations, I was obliged to cook. This I could only do by racial memory. I had never before gone further than to make toast when the bread had become too green to eat raw. Now I found myself clawing away at the carcases of dead animals until my nails were full of blood and I felt like a mangy old eagle.

Washing up could still be kept to one operation a week

if I never tried to pass the fish barrier but ate fish, if at all, only on Sunday evening.

I found that I had become so spinsterish that I was made neurotic not only by my life of domesticity but by the slightest derangement of my room. I would burst into a fit of weeping if the kettle was not facing due east. My efforts at self-control completely exhausted me but I knew that if I ever said with the faintest asperity such words as 'Oh, do be quiet!' or 'Don't put your feet up there!', one or other of us would have to join the Foreign Legion.

Though the situation often got out of hand, my friend was never rebellious, but there were times when the realization swept over him that I was all he'd got. Then he hated me.

I got shingles. My skin hung down over one side of my rib-cage like the wall-paper in my room. Yet I was only bearing two-sevenths of the weight that lies for a lifetime on the shoulders of the average married woman. I had to face the fact that as tender comrade, faithful friend, I was a dead loss.

These unpleasant facts about my own character were but grim confirmation of long-held suspicions. What I learned about the rest of the human race through my association with Barn Door was a startling revelation, but I have no doubt that in knowing him I came to know the whole world.

There is no great dark man.

Even under an exterior as rugged as a mountain range, there lurks the same wounded, wincing psyche that cripples the rest of us. Where we are led to think we will find strength, we shall discover force; where we hope for ruthlessness, we shall unearth spite; and when we think we are clinging desperately to a rock, it is falling upon us. Even with a man whose neck is thicker than his head, if we are not careful, we shall be involved in an argument about who most loves whom. The trouble is that, if you find that by mistake you have bitten into a soft centre, you can't very well put it back in the box.

A little old lady once said to me, 'I have known a great many men. All of them had to be carried every step of the way.'

This was true of my friend. He could hardly stand, let alone totter forward under his burdens. They were no less heavy for being imaginary.

In a heartless hoax practised upon innocent dragonflies, entomologists laughingly placed the tails in the mouths of some of these creatures. The insects gratefully ate their nether extremities as far up as they could reach. They then died. This was the stage of evolution at which my friend had remained. When I gave him a nail file he used it on his toenails until they sank below the horizon; then he filed his toes. This and other similar happenings at first gave me the idea that he was a divinely rudimentary being. If he was it did not save him from being painfully aware of his unenviable position in society, rendered no better by knowing me. About this he could never make up his mind what to do. Sometimes he walked several yards behind me so as to be able to send me up for the amusement of passers-by; at others he made unprovoked protestations of friendship in the presence of strangers who happened to be sitting at our table in a café. In spite of spending so much time among hooligans he conceived of himself as being poorer and of lower degree than his acquaintances and felt that these handicaps caused him to be alone in the world. I pointed out that he spent his week-ends with me, his days with his workmates and his nights flailing his arms and singing snatches of opera in various cafés crowded to the walls. None of these activities assuaged his feeling of isolation. Its real cause was his inability to take an interest in other people. No one had ever taught him how.

His greatest burden was time. Now for the first time I understood the true purpose of the radio, in the wailing, crooning, stuttering stream of which he bathed himself every waking hour. Its function is not to entertain but to drown the ticking of all clocks. Having, myself, spent so many happy hours alone, frequently doing nothing but breathing, I was bewildered to discover that for my friend spare time was an imposition. If one event, say Sunday lunch, ended before another such as the movies could begin, he became distraught. He cleaned his shoes – yea, though they were already like crimson glass. He put a new flint in his lighter and he twiddled the whistling, creaking, crackling knobs of our crotchety wireless set but, though he spent his days picking and shovelling, the one thing he never did was to sit and dream. In this respect I would have been tempted to say that he was ill did I not know that health consists of having the same diseases as one's neighbours.

Chapter Twenty-two

There had to be another war. The sadness of the First World War and the sweetness of songs like 'There's a Long, Long Trail' were qualities memory had bestowed on experiences that at the time were colourless. While I lived through them, if I noticed anything except the men in uniform, it was a slight lack of variety in the food. My prep schoolmaster once told the class I was in that it was part of the air-raid generation. I tried to look deprived but I had no clear notion of how to act out the distinction his words gave us.

Perhaps it was because the First World War had left me so unmoved that I did not take the second one very seriously. When news reached me in 1940 that London was burning I was sitting in a cottage outside Basingstoke with a pregnant actress. I had nothing to lose but my aerograph and my typewriter but, explaining that I ought to spread my brooding pinions over these, I rushed home. The truth was that I couldn't bear to miss the great drama of my time.

Back in the city I noticed at once that, though some of the buildings had been ruined, most of the people had been improved. Everyone talked to everyone – even to me. The golden age had temporarily arrived.

Even before this, my position in society had undergone a change for reasons over which I had no control. The women of London had gone butch. At all ages and on every social level, they had taken to uniforms – or near-uniforms. They wore jackets, trousers and sensible shoes. I could now buy easily the footwear that I had always favoured – black lace-up shoes with firm, medium heels. I became indistinguishable from a woman.

Once, as I stood at a bus stop, a policeman accused me of this. After looking me up and down for nearly a minute he asked me what I was doing.

Me: I'm waiting for a bus.

Policeman: You're dressed as a woman.

Me (amazed): I'm wearing trousers.

Policeman: Women wear trousers.

Me: Are you blaming me because everybody else is so eccentric?

Policeman (louder): You're dressed as a woman and you'd better catch a bus quick or there will be trouble. People don't like that sort of thing (pointing at my flyless trousers and my high-heeled shoes).

The policeman was right. People did not like that sort of thing and could now add patriotism to their other less easily named reasons for hating me. It was only superficially and only by day that strangers were friendly. Throughout the war I was at times in very unpleasant situations. The difficulty was to pass from a place where I could be clearly seen into the black-out without being followed. I did not always manage this.

As I was standing in an Underground train on my way to Tottenham Court Road Station, the nearest stop to Fitzrovia, some men left their seats and came to have a closer look at me. They stood around discussing my private life in public voices. Then one of them put his hand on the front of my trousers and said, 'Yes, he has got something there. It is a man.'

At Holborn Station I waited until the doors of the train

were about to shut. Then I darted out on to the platform, but one of the men must have managed to wedge his foot in between the closing doors. As I ran up the escalator, I could hear feet pounding the stairs behind me. I should not have gone out into the street. It placed me, when I turned round, in a position where my pursuers could see me better than I could see them. This time they hit me with a weapon of some kind or hammered my face against the wall or else I fell very heavily as I lost consciousness. Certainly the damage was worse than usual. As soon as I came to, I stood up to avoid being trampled on by accident and, as usual in such situations, counted my fingernails and felt my teeth with my tongue. They were all present and correct but my face was bleeding. Holding my handkerchief to my nose, I began to walk home. I couldn't go back into the Underground station. I had no idea what I looked like.

After an evening class in Willesden I was returning to real life by bus. From the top front seat I saw an Australian soldier standing in the queue at Notting Hill Gate. Even in the black-out I recognized his road-sweeper's hat. As the bus moved forward again, using the darkened window before me as a mirror, I noticed that this man had seated himself immediately behind me. A moment later I felt his hand solemnly placed on my head. I sat motionless, never taking my eyes from the window. Presently I saw his reflection take from its pocket a comb. At this point I guessed that whatever was going to happen would not involve violence. For the rest of the journey to Hyde Park Corner, the soldier sat quietly and combed my hair. I do not think he can have been drunk. He could understand the architecture of my coiffure which baffled many total abstainers.

Australia must be a strange country. It is the home of the kangaroo, the duck-billed platypus and the hair-comber.

Sometimes when I told this tale in Toni's someone would say, 'Can't have had any idea you were really a man!' On other occasions the comment was, 'Must have known you weren't a woman.'

The black-out was almost never really black. One night, when London was filled with a dense fog, I remember that it became necessary for me to creep along with outstretched hands feeling brickwork, railings and passers-by in an effort to keep my bearings. The rest of the time, even in winter, I did not have to diminish my pace or even watch the ground at my feet. I never fell down and seldom crashed into anything.

On one of these twilit nights I was sweeping along Ebury Street when a tall bearded silhouette passed me by. I could not put up with that so I stopped. The stranger retraced his steps to where I stood. 'Who are you?' I asked and he replied, 'I am Angus McBean. Who are you?' I hurriedly explained that I was nobody but added, as an extenuating circumstance, that I knew plenty of people to whom his name was sacred. There and then he said he would photograph me. When I told him that I never paid for anything he did not withdraw his offer. A few evenings later he took about a dozen pictures of me in three-quarters of an hour.

Even if we had not met in Ebury Street, I feel that we would have met somewhere sooner or later. Though it was something that he did every day of his life, Mr McBean longed to take photographs as fervently as I desired to be photographed. He worked very quickly and methodically, his instructions as clear as lenses. 'Lick your lower lip and let it hang' and, the moment before the camera clicked, 'Pull your ears back.' When I asked him what portrait photography was all about he said, 'It's simple. They want to be beautiful.' To this end, even on great beauties, every surface that was at half moon – that was passing from light to dark – was retouched from the texture of an orange to the smoothness of an apple. With some of his sitters everything was retouched but their titles. One woman, while he was deciding what on earth to do with her, snatched up in both hands the swags of superfluous flesh that encumbered her jaw-bones and said, 'You do understand, don't you, that all this is not part of the essential me.'

Perhaps the best exposition of his technique is contained in this story. Dandy Nichols, the cockney comedienne, when I mentioned Mr McBean's name, said, 'I must go to Angus and have some mugs done.' Later I asked him if a certain Miss Nichols had visited his studio to 'have some mugs done'. 'I saw that was what she had come for,' he replied, 'but I did cups and saucers.'

Of the pictures he took of me, my friends said, 'I see you can go down to history as a famous beauty whatever you happen to look like.'

The recipe for success that I had seen in the life of Mr Cross I now witnessed again in the boundless energy of Mr McBean. At eleven at night when I was departing, he was just beginning to make props, mount prints and construct surreal backgrounds for actresses to lie on, lie under, sit in or poke their heads through.

In obedience to that force in my nature that drove me long ago to pass from admitting that I was homosexual to protesting the fact, my slightly British determination to ignore the hazards of wartime London soon became a desire to embrace disaster. It was fear that was the lure. All other emotions I had to work up artificially. I could never be sure whether I felt them or only wished that I did. When I was afraid I knew the sensation was genuine. As soon as the bombardment of London began I felt totally engaged.

When the ground began to shake and the sky became pink with doom I could hardly stay at home. I ceased to go out only when it was necessary and started to search London for my own true bomb.

Among the places which could be used as a pretext for crossing the city in an air raid was the flat in Russell Court that my art student friend shared with the Czech. I visited her unmercifully until, one day, she telephoned me to implore me not to come as the Czech seemed to be on the fringe of a nervous breakdown.

I should have foreseen this but I did not. In the company I kept a man would have to behave very oddly indeed before his friends would call in a doctor. We all attributed the Czech's eccentricity to his nationality.

After a while he took to standing all night with his back to the wall, his gaze fixed on the door in case *they* should come in. His girl-friend could not do otherwise than commit him to a mental hospital.

The war did not cause his madness. It aggravated it by pressing on the soft wall of a hopelessly unrealistic personality. In order to enjoy the war it was essential to be tough – and lucky.

For most of 1940 London by night was like one of those dimly-lit parties that their hosts hope are slightly wicked. In a cosy gloom young men and women strolled arm in arm along Piccadilly murmuring, 'It's not as bad tonight as last night, is it?' Policemen allowed themselves a certain skittishness. 'Don't care, huh?' they cried as I passed them sheltering in doorways. Taxi-drivers unbent so far as to take one part of the way home free of charge. As soon as bombs started to fall, the city became like a paved double bed. Voices whispered suggestively to you as you walked along; hands reached out if you stood still and in dimly lit trains people carried on as they had once behaved only in taxis. I was only becoming aware that railway carriages were the playgrounds of exhibitionists now that I spent so many hours a week travelling to and from art schools in the Home Counties. I was surprised at the frequency with which I found myself sitting opposite some man who between stations decided to try to win fame, like Mr Mercator, for his projection. The insult implied in these offers of instant sex no longer troubled me. I was worried because I knew so well that what seemed to be starting out as a frolic might easily turn into something quite different. I realized too that if any unpleasantness occurred, so far from being able to enlist anyone's sympathy, I should be considered to have caused it. Neither distaste nor apprehension must be displayed at such a moment. As I hope all compendiums for young ladies tell their readers, it is best to adopt a completely matter-of-fact air and, feigning a yawn, to say, 'Oh, put it away.'

Outside railway trains, overtures made possible by the black-out – though hardly delicate – were at least a little more romantic.

Once, when I emerged from Leicester Square Underground station, the outline of the buildings on the opposite side of the road looked so unfamiliar that I thought I must have taken the wrong exit. When I asked an invisible passer-by where I was, he kissed me on the lips, told me I was in Newport Street and walked on.

By heterosexuals the life after death is imagined as a world of light, where there is no parting. If there is a heaven for homosexuals, which doesn't seem very likely, it will be very poorly lit and full of people they can feel pretty confident they will never have to meet again. It is only partly because they are ashamed of themselves and wish to remain unrecognized that this environment seems so desirable. The chief reason is that it makes possible contacts of astounding physical intimacy without the intervention of personality. To either partner, the other is a phallus garlanded with fantasies, chiefly of masculinity. The homosexual world is a world of spinsters. Most homosexuals over the age of twenty-five will play, on the physical level, an active, passive or unspecified role with the same or a different partner from night to night or even from hour to hour, but emotionally they search perpetually for a real man who desires passionately (as opposed to making do with) another man. This being, if he exists, is so rare that one might as well enter a monastery on reaching puberty. The less drastic alternative is to live a real sex life in a dream world. This can best be done in the dark with strangers.

Playgrounds where these circumstances obtain are not easy to find. When discovered they are frequented first by the few, later by the many and finally by the police. At one time the towpath at Putney was such a dreamland, but it became so well known that the police took to driving motor launches along that part of the river and suddenly shining searchlights on its southern bank. When this happened everyone who was not already in that position flung himself flat on the ground.

As this riverside brothel declined in popularity Whitstone Pond on Hampstead Heath became all the rage. More foliage abounded there. This lent a certain sylvan charm and some useful escape routes. Now there is a certain cinema in London where it is said that all the films shown have a 'Q' certificate (no normal person may be admitted to any part of this programme unless accompanied by a homosexual). It hardly matters what films are exhibited. War films are the type most frequently shown: their sound-tracks help to conceal the noise of creaking seat springs. Movies which have extensive snow scenes are avoided as these cast too much light back into the auditorium. During the war,

159

however, this cinema was almost empty and the river bank at Putney became a desert. The whole of London was one long towpath, one vast movie house.

I had always shunned these homosexual playgrounds; less from purity than vanity. I did not want a liaison in conditions which might tend to obliterate my individuality. On this subject the last word must go to a Canadian actress who said, 'If the fuss is not about ourselves, then what the hell?'

Then suddenly, into this feast of love and death that St Adolf had set before the palates of the English – parched these long dark twenty-five years – Mr Roosevelt began, with Olympian hands, to shower the American forces. This brand new army of (no) occupation flowed through the streets of London like cream on strawberries, like melted butter over green peas. Labelled 'with love from Uncle Sam' and packaged in uniforms so tight that in them their owners could fight for nothing but their honour, these 'bundles for Britain' leaned against the lamp-posts of Shaftesbury Avenue or lolled on the steps of thin-lipped statues of dead English statesmen. As they sat in the cafés or stood in the pubs, their bodies bulged through every straining khaki fibre towards our feverish hands. Their voices were like warm milk, their skins as flawless as expensive indiarubber, and their eyes as beautiful as glass. Above all it was the liberality of their natures that was so marvellous. Never in the history of sex was so much offered to so many by so few. At the first gesture of acceptance from a stranger, words of love began to ooze from their lips, sexuality from their bodies and pound notes from their pockets like juice from a peeled peach.

The obliquity of the English was something to which I had been accustomed from childhood. My father was a living – well, an example of it. Taught by him I had walked all my life in the excruciating armour of self-restraint. I was, therefore, never more than mildly surprised at the hedging antics of strangers who followed me in the street. They would sometimes walk behind me for half an hour, quickening their pace if I hurried, slackening it if I dawdled and crossing over the road when I did, as though we were playing Follow-my-leader. If, to avoid any further waste of their time, I turned and politely explained that I was a dead loss, they would snort with indignation and say, 'I don't know what you mean.' It was the directness of the Americans that astonished me. Apparently from the 49th parallel to the Gulf of Mexico face-saving is unknown. These young men walked, not behind, but beside you and at once began a conversation with some such words as 'You and me's interested in the same things, I guess.' If you wanted, like Madam Butterfly, 'a little bit to tease them' and said, 'But I'm interested in the life of the spirit,' they replied, 'Me too.' If they were rejected without equivocation, they accepted the fact good-naturedly. Even when it was obvious that they had mistaken me for a woman, they allowed themselves to be enlightened with no display of disgust.

American: Can I walk you home, ma'am?

Me: You think I'm a woman, don't you?

American: You waggle your fanny like a woman.

Me: Oh, I should ignore that.

American: I'm trying to but it's not that easy.

Conversations such as this told me that I was by nature American. To the rest of the world happiness was a suspiciously regarded by-product of some other pursuit (preferably noble). Americans and homosexuals sought it for its own sake. The Portuguese explorers of old set out across the Atlantic Ocean in search of the Islands of the Blessed. They were not mocked. If the golden age flourishes anywhere it is in the United States.

By the time the last Americans had vanished into thin Englishmen I was nearly forty.

While the G.I.s were still around, I lived almost every moment that I spent out of doors in a state of exhilaration. It was my nature to deploy my forces in breadth, so at first I was content to know many soldiers superficially, but after a while I decided to change my strategy to one of depth and concentrate on a single individual. You can't have your cake and not eat it.

Never before had a physical relationship been presented to me so completely without stint and without overtones.

Sex is generally processed in one of three shades. It may be crude, which leads to the numbing repetition of the shortest words for the longest things, or naughty, involving one or both or all parties in dressing up, or it may be poetic. This was the tint favoured by me in my youth – it transforms the facts of life into an ego-boosting device. Americans serve it plain but, sad to say, about the physical practice of homosexual intercourse there tends to be something contrived. This robs the act of its function as a means of communication. The two participants will never be of one flesh. When I was moaning about this to a Lesbian friend, she drew in her elbows and, with her face contorted in a grimace of disgust, asked, 'Who wants to be of one flesh with anybody?' I think that initially most homosexuals do. To outsiders the idea that between a man and a woman the sex act can be natural, unnamed, inevitable and lead to total oneness gives normality the radiance of the Holy Grail. Only a lifetime of receiving the confidences of unhappily married middle-aged women brought me to the realization that in time, even for heterosexuals, sex is reduced to an indoor sport. This was consoling. It is nice to be in the same boat as one's betters especially if it is sinking.

For the practical level of human contact I was now prepared and I was happy but, of course, no more so than if I had met someone who could do a Ximenes crossword or play chess at my shaky standard. I learned to like my American but would never have put his interests before those of my lifelong friends and he would not have expected me to. I was always pleased to see him but would have left him with no more than a sigh for a steady income, a job in the movie industry or a man who weighed twice as much. I could not have said that I loved him. When he ceased to call on me, I had no idea whether he had gone to heaven or to New York – but, then, to me they were the same place.

When the Spartans burst into Troy, the women of the city hid themselves in conspicuous places and screamed if they were not observed. Similar antics were now performed by English girls. This I recognized was mere coyness in the face of a frontal attack but I could not help noticing that, among my friends, my adoration for Americans was not wholeheartedly shared. The behaviour of those who wished to be thought highbrow bordered on discourtesy. One night as I was sitting in the Wheatsheaf, an American soldier leaned with both hands on the table in front of me and asked, 'Are you by any chance a celebrity?' With downcast eyes I explained that I was not but that I would introduce him to some. Rising and leaving the nonentities with whom I had been sitting snorting behind me, I led the culture-seeker to Nina Hamnett, explaining that she had known Modigliani. She was leaning her laughing torso against the bar. 'Miss Hamnett,' I said, 'allow me to present an American who wishes to meet a celebrity.' I then started on a list of her claims to fame as though she were a public monument and I a tourists' guide. 'Is he going to buy me a drink?' she said. This he promptly did but she remained obviously displeased with both of us. I found this hard to understand. All she was now being asked to do was make like a genius for a few minutes. It took a lot more coaxing from me and a lot more drink from the soldier to persuade her to do this. In the end our persistence was rewarded. She told us one of her best stories.

A friend of hers sent a statue of a nude boy that she had modelled in black wax to an art gallery in Derby. Black wax is soft and, before you could say 'Sex', the figure had been robbed of what some would consider the most important part of its anatomy. When this vandalism came to the notice of Miss Hamnett's friend she complained to the municipal body that she considered responsible. They replied that the loss sustained by the statue came under the heading of fair wear and tear.

I secretly preferred the cafés of Charlotte Street to its public houses and, on the days when I had no work at all to do, would gladly have drunk pale-grey coffees from midday to midnight if I could have found people to listen when I spoke; but life in that part of the world was tidal. At six o'clock every evening the nomadic tribes moved south to the Wheatsheaf, the Marquis of Granby and the Bricklayers Arms. The northern regions became depopulated.

Drink and the world drinks with you; eat and you eat alone. I regretted the truth of this maxim because the life of pubs is never as gay as the life of cafés. As at a party so in the Wheatsheaf, unless I arrived within an hour of opening time I found the deadening effect of alcohol had begun to work on everyone present. Some had become sleepy; some had become surly; and Mr Tambimuttu had become Spanish and was dancing it off. Conversation did not flow with the drink; it drowned in it. This did not produce silence, for some drinkers erroneously imagined that they had become wiser and wittier and consequently spoke louder than usual.

These pubs, these cafés and the space between them were Fitzrovia – that kingdom afterwards to be described so well by Roland Camberton in a novel called *Scamp* and later still by Maclaren-Ross in his memoirs. As though we had some foreknowledge that we were living literature, we all set to work to be cameos. We tried with significant gestures and memorable phrases to give good value for the welcome that I at any rate was so surprised to find that we received.

What was required was a bizarre idiom that was completely consistent within itself. Of all the natives of Fitzrovia only one person really had this qualification. The suit she was calling was fallen grandeur and in it she never missed a trick.

A day came when this woman found in a dustbin in Bond Street a backless bead frock. No sooner had she seen it than she longed to wear it. As she did not at that time live anywhere in particular, it was difficult to think of a place sufficiently secluded for trying it on. She chose the churchyard in Flitcroft Street and sat among the dead to wait for nightfall. When it was barely dusk her eagerness had overcome her prudence. She started her impromptu striptease performance. A crowd collected large enough to attract the attention of the police and she was led away.

The next morning when the magistrate asked her what she had been doing, with a gently mocking laugh at the uncouthness of the question she replied, 'What any woman would be doing at that hour. Changing for dinner.'

Though we never stopped trying, none of us ever achieved such high style as this, but converting one's life into a form of public entertainment turned out to be less difficult than I had imagined.

I had feared that I might run out of quips, gags, anecdotes and epigrams and, on the way back to London from Watford, Willesden or Woolwich, worked assiduously on my material. This was effort wasted. If the aesthetic posture of my youth had not forced me to show the utmost contempt for the music halls, I might long ago have learned that what audiences most want to hear is what they already know, so that even newcomers may know that the lines are stale and may enjoy the idiocy forced upon the comedian by his profession. It is only to remarks that were not funny even in the first instance that a performer must endeavour to give some kind of sparkle. In the last resort he, himself, must laugh.

With practice it became easier to deck out my discourse with these tricks than not, and soon what had once been my café technique became my only manner of speaking. In middle age I found that I had gone beyond my original aim of purging my speech of the dross of sincerity. I had robbed it of all meaning whatsoever. I became like a stopped clock. I was right about once every twelve years, but what good was that when everyone had ceased to look at my face? To people who knew me well, listening to me became almost unbearable. In some houses I was only welcome if I undertook not to utter the same catch-phrases more than twice in any one evening. I tried to stay within bounds but really there was nothing for others to do but listen, act as stooges or leave.

Among those who often came to Toni's and had sufficient vitality to wade into the torrent of my volubility was a certain Mr MacQueen. The moment that he learned that I was a lettering artist, he hired me, though when he uttered the words he had not even formed a company. All he had was a tiny house on Campden Hill on which the paint was not yet dry and a head full of ideas in an equally unusable state. He proposed to start a firm that would build exhibition stands, decorate showrooms and construct display units. I don't really hold with exhibitions unless they are of myself but I graciously accepted the wages he paid me. I also helped him engage other members of the staff. This frequently entailed interviewing art students and looking at drawings of myself curled round window poles. It was while I was in Mr MacQueen's employ that I was arrested.

Chapter Twenty-three

❧

This was an eventuality that I and my enemies had expected ever since the far-off days when I had first been questioned by the police. A young man called Bermondsey Lizzie had once said, 'You'll get years one of these days, girl, but you'll tell them everything, won't you? – when you come up for trial, I mean. I'll never forgive you if you don't.'

Being in a display firm is like working for the movie industry. When you are not coping with a crisis you are wondering how on earth to fill in your time. During one of these lulls I was given a day off. I decided to spend this buying a pair of shoes. This was always a difficult and dangerous mission for me. If I wanted to use the longest words for the shortest thing I would say that I was a passive foot fetishist. My feet were smaller than an ordinary mortal's and I wanted everyone to know this. As time went by I wore shorter and shorter shoes, not because the length of my feet decreased but because the amount of discomfort I could bear became greater. Finally I was able to endure footwear that was hardly visible to the naked eye. For me, as for Hans Andersen's little mermaid, every step was agony but as she had finally been rewarded by dancing with a prince, I never gave up. Almost as uncomfortable as wearing the shoes was buying them. Both I and the shop assistant needed all the fortitude we could summon. I would describe the shoes I had in mind and ask for a size four. The salesman or woman (according to what sex the management had decided I was) would measure my foot and bring me a shoe that fitted me perfectly. This immediately aroused my suspicion. When I ripped it off and looked at the sole, I found it to be a six. Moving down the scale in semitones, I would try on successive sizes until my toes were folded inside the shoe like the leaves of an artichoke. Then I would say, 'Now lift me up.' If I could stand in them, those were the shoes I bought. Tottering into the street, I screamed for a taxi. To this day my feet are two mis-shapen plinths of twisted bone.

Since I knew what an ordeal awaited me once I had entered a shoe shop, I did not do so lightly. I scrutinized the goods in the window until I was sure what I wanted was inside. This was what I was doing on the fatal afternoon. I had already systematically searched all the likely windows in Oxford Street and was just starting on Charing Cross Road when I was stopped by two policemen disguised as human beings. They demanded to see my exemption papers. As always I showed them the one that said that I suffered from sexual perversion. When my inquisitors had retrieved their eyebrows from the roots of their hair, they gave me back this by now rather grubby document and I moved on.

Outside the Hippodrome Theatre I met by chance a certain part-time hooligan called Mr Palmer. I slapped on to his plate his ration of eternal wisdom for the day and turned into Coventry Street. Almost immediately I was stopped a second time by the same two men. 'Just a moment, you,' they said. 'We are taking you in for soliciting.'

I marched before them following the instructions they muttered to me from behind. These led to Savile Row police station where I was searched by one man while others stood round saying, 'Mind how you go.' I was not stripped, but my pockets were emptied and I was sufficiently unzipped for it to be seen that I was not wearing women's underclothes. Then I was asked if I minded having my finger-prints taken. I replied that it couldn't matter less. To this day, my prints lie in the files of Scotland Yard and just beyond them there are ten little squiggles that I expect Edgar Lustgarten sits up nights pondering over. They are the marks of my fingernails, which it had not been possible to keep out of the ink.

The police did not start to be really irritating until the question arose of finding someone to go bail for me. This was necessary so that I could by telephone distribute my most immediate bookings in the schools among the various models and warn Mr MacQueen that I would not be at work the next day or possibly for six months to come. If all this had not been necessary, I would quite contentedly have spent the night in the police station. I can sleep anywhere. I offered to supply a list of names, addresses and telephone numbers and the money for making the calls so that someone might quickly be found who was free to come to Savile Row. This they would not allow me to do. 'Just give us one name,' they said stubbornly. So I gave the ballet teacher, on whom they called several times without finding her in. At about ten at night they asked me for the name of another person and I gave them that of the man who had written the Kangaroo limerick. Fortunately he arrived almost immediately. I dashed through the blacked-out streets of London, first to Mr Palmer. He was the young man to whom I had been seen speaking in the street during the afternoon. I asked him (if he could get time off from work) to come to court the following morning and say that he knew me. Then I went on to Toni's to tell the world in case anyone was interested in seeing foul play. Finally I reached home and made countless telephone calls, some offering speaking parts to friends of long standing who could act as character witnesses, and others to people who might like to appear as crowd artists. The next day, dressed in black so as to maintain the great tradition, I set out with my entourage for Bow Street.

As soon as I stepped into the courtroom, I was assailed by two contrary feelings. The first was that here was the long awaited fully involving situation to which I could summon all my capacity for survival. The second was that I might fall on the floor in a dead faint and that it might be just as well if I did.

In the days when I knew the Irish and the Scottish boys, I was often in police courts to act as a chorus to them or their friends and to cry 'Woe unto Ilium' if an unfair verdict was given, but as soon as I, myself, was on trial, I found that I knew nothing of the judicial ritual. I had not, for instance, remembered that the magistrate sits in a state of patient trance while the case against you is conducted by his clerk.

I marvelled at the benignity of the magistrate, who himself instructed me in the procedure of the court, and I was appalled by his clerk's bitchiness. He played the whole scene for laughs, turning slowly towards the public, with his hands in the air like George Sanders uttering his best lines. These included, 'You are a male person, I presume.' This total abandonment of dignity reminded me of the collapse of Harley Street at my medical examination four years earlier.

The police behaved in the perfectly conventional way that I remembered well. They rattled off their evidence as though it were the litany. They said that between the hours of this and that, they had observed the accused stopping and speaking to various people who had looked horrified and torn themselves away. At one moment they included in this great work of fiction a touch of realism.

They mentioned the young man with whom I had talked outside the Hippodrome.

When the police had completed their evidence, the magistrate asked me if I would prefer to reply from the dock or go into the witness box where I would have to take the oath. I chose the latter, not because I hoped to gain anything from invoking the aid of You-Know-Who but because it would raise me to a higher vantage point and, like posing on a rostrum in an art school, lend me a spurious nobility. It also meant that I did not have my back to the audience for the whole of my big scene, which I had decided to play dead straight like Imogen in *Cymbeline*.

I forbore to state that the two policemen who had arrested me were inveterate liars. I humbly put forward the opinion that they had drawn mistaken conclusions from what they saw and that their error had been prompted by their having read my exemption paper which described me as homosexual. This they had not mentioned in their evidence. I also suggested that they might have misinterpreted my appearance. I said that I dressed and lived in such a way that the whole world could see that I was homosexual but that this set me apart from the rest of humanity rather than making it easy for me to form contacts with it. Who, I asked the magistrate, could possibly hope to solicit anybody in broad daylight in a crowded London street looking as I did?

At this point, I was later told by one of my friends who was sitting in the court, a stranger whispered, 'They can't do nothing with 'im. He can't 'elp 'isself. You can see that.'

This we all agreed marked the dawn of a new day.

Various kind people gave evidence as to the irreproachability of my character and, to my relief, Mr Palmer went into the witness box to declare that he had spoken to me the previous afternoon because he knew me. He was nervous, but he spoke clearly and without hesitation. That he had secret reserves of courage I did not at that time know. I only discovered that ten years later when, at about the age of thirty-two, he committed suicide. Everyone who spoke on my behalf was asked by the magistrate's clerk if he knew that I was homosexual and replied that he did. This question was in each case followed immediately by the words, uttered in a voice hoarse with incredulity, 'And yet you describe him as respectable?' All said, 'Yes.'

When the magistrate tired of this recital of my praises he said that the evidence against me was insufficient to convict me. I was dismissed. He meant that the evidence was a lie. If it had been true, it could have caused the downfall of an archbishop.

Everyone who was present at my trial or who was told about it later was amazed at my acquittal. One friend, fearing the worst, had advised me to try to have my case postponed while I engaged the services of a lawyer. This would incidentally have brought up one of the nastier points of the law. If I did this and then lost my case, I must take it for granted that my sentence would be heavier. In other words Justice revenges herself not only on those who commit crimes but also on those who take up her time. I decided against seeking legal aid not because I feared that my time in jail might be prolonged but because my case did not seem to require the help of 'my learned friend'. There were no subtle legal points to be argued. Unless the accused produces an alibi there never can be evidence of a person not speaking to strangers. I felt that if I clearly protested my innocence it should be effective. I also feared that a lawyer might deliberately blur the issue of my being homosexual on the quite logical ground that it was not the point. Whether it was relevant or not, my one desire was to state in a court of law that I was homosexual and as stainless as Sheffield steel. This was a distinction that, ten years earlier, would have been very difficult to make, but this magistrate at least had seen that this might be so.

The police, as usual, merely wanted a conviction. They thought that their case simply could not go wrong once I had been seen in court. This scramble to gain promotion by securing a large number of arrests is an unpleasant part of the police system, but I could not say that, either in this case in particular or throughout my life generally, the police have treated me badly. What made me feel so unremittingly hostile towards them was their facetiousness and the insulting manner displayed by a group of people who should at all costs remain neutral.

When they arrested me they could only be accused of stating a little more than they could prove. They followed a known homosexual who stopped several times (possibly pretending) to look in shop windows. Whenever I stopped a small crowd collected. I don't remember the details of that afternoon but it would be safe to assume that a few remarks were made to me or at me. Unless constables were standing between me and whoever was speaking they would not be able to say for certain whether I replied or not. Their crime was that they swore I had and implied that I had spoken first. I could swear that I did not speak first to anyone because I never did. I could be fairly certain that I did not answer at all because remarks uttered by strangers, unless they are made in an American accent, always contained a veiled or a naked insult. So I was technically not guilty and, at the time, felt appropriately outraged. Yet if there are degrees of innocence, I would not now claim to have won first class honours. My thoughts on this subject are vague because I am not sure what the laws against soliciting are framed to prevent. If soliciting is a crime because it is a nuisance to those who do not wish to be importuned, then not only I but most homosexuals are guiltless. Very few men would dare to annoy strangers by detaining them against their will or even continuing to speak to them if the slightest irritation were evinced. Is soliciting criminal because it is the first step in the procedure of prostitution? This can less be taken for granted in a homosexual context than in any other. Many men make overtures to others without any thought of receiving or parting with money.

Of all these charges I would claim to be not guilty but how innocent am I?

I do not solicit for immoral purposes because it would be unfeminine – and risky – but perhaps my very existence is a form of importuning. I no longer ask strange men for money because I do not think I would get it but, if it were offered to me, I would not feel ashamed to take it. In the last analysis I cannot say that I have ever refrained from taking any course of action on the ground that it was wrong or illegal or immoral.

Chapter Twenty-four

❧

When the trial was over I went back for about a year to
work for the display expert. He had sent a note to the court
expressing his confidence in me and he continued to employ
me as though nothing disgraceful had happened. The police
were not equally magnanimous. They began systematically
to make sure that I was barred from the public houses of
Fitzrovia – finally, to everyone's amazement, even from the
Wheatsheaf. My friends protested hotly to the landlord.
He coolly pointed out that he could not have a licence
and me. In the past four years he had observed so much
eccentricity that my presence made very little difference,
but the police had accused him of running 'a funny kind
of place' and, when he had said, 'How funny?' they had
pointed to me. I was compelled to take the veil of abstinence
which suited me quite well, but I also had to relinquish half
my audience which did not. At first I complained volubly at
this narrowing of my kingdom, but gradually snorts gave
place to tears as I realized that this was but part of a
gradual lessening of scope to which time was just starting
to subject me.

Peace broke out.

On that terrible evening, as I was weaving my way
through the West End with a prolonged 'grand chain'
movement as though I were doing the lancers with the
whole world, my name was called. I heard it above the
shouting, laughing, singing that went on all that night.

Turning I saw in a doorway the man who had put up with my airs and graces all those long, horrible months in Baron's Court when I had first come to London fourteen years earlier.

I paused questioningly in front of him. He said, 'You look terrible.'

The horrors of peace were many.

Death-made-easy vanished overnight and soon love-made-easy, personified by the American soldiers, also disappeared. At a Christmas party in one of the rooms in our house a woman entered and embraced me. Over her shoulder I saw, hesitating in the doorway, a G.I. The woman said brightly, 'I brought him for you. He's a bit small but they're getting difficult to find. Come in, Ricky.'

But not only did love and death become rationed. Even mere friendship grew scarce. Londoners started to regret their indiscriminate expansiveness. People do when some moment of shared danger is past. Emotions that had been displayed had now to be lived down; confidences had been uttered which must now be gainsaid. I, who had once been a landmark more cheerful looking and more bomb-proof than St Paul's Cathedral, had ceased to be a talisman. I had become a loathsome reminder of the unfairness of fate. I was still living while the young, the brave and the beautiful were dead.

All these external changes came at a bad time for me when they could add their weight to other unwelcome alterations that were taking place within.

I was growing old.

My friends were delighted and did not resist the temptation occasionally to nudge me towards the grave with a straight talk. A teacher of languages called Lamb Chop came further out into the open than most others. He said, 'You are dyeing your hair in order to seem younger.' This was untrue. I had started to use henna when I was twenty-four but as my life was one long journey towards self-assessment, I felt I must always give consideration to the opinions of me held by other people however malicious I might secretly think them. Since I had adopted my chi-chi appearance partly as propaganda, if the message became confused, I must alter it. I set about forcing red out and forcing blue in. This would continue my original purpose of showing that my hair was dyed but would allow it to be seen that, underneath the tinting, I was grey-haired.

The moment that I had decided upon this course of action – long before I had begun to put it into practice on my fortieth birthday in 1948 – my entire body went into revolt. My face became blistered with a crimson rash. It irritated so much that the effort not to claw myself to pieces was totally exhausting. As soon as the red marks began to appear the only thing to do was to go home and lie down in the dark – preferably in a draught. After a day or two the redness would begin to subside and the places where it had been to dry and harden into white scales. Within five days the skin of my face had fallen to the ground with a clatter leaving the surface beneath as good as new. Then the whole process would begin again. This illness continued for a whole summer. It was said by my friends to be caused by an allergy. If so it was an allergy to middle age. I never recovered. For ever after I could only keep the disfigurement quiescent if I was awash with cortisone and pickled with anti-histamine.

During a shaky transition state which lasted for about six months, I passed from doubtful youth to unmistakable middle age. I became one of the stately homos of England. This was the result in me of entering my blue period. On others the effect was equally marked. For many years after the war I was never badly savaged by members of the public nor even directly insulted by them. This was not because anyone had seen the light. Abatement in the hostility of one's enemies must never be thought to signify that they have been won over. It only means that one has ceased to constitute a threat. The attitude towards me of strangers waned from fear to brutish contempt. Without my scarlet hair I was like a Westerner without a gun.

I was growing old.

A day came when, on leaving the café that was fashionable with hooligans at the time, I saw that it was raining. During the war a flood would not have deterred me from proceeding on foot. Now I took the weather to be a sign and that evening I travelled home by bus, resolving to do this from then on.

As I took a seat on the upper deck, a stranger said, 'Too wet even for you?'

A year or two after this, I was made aware that I was not only a characteristic of the night life of London but that my name had become an international rate of exchange.

As he wandered through the streets of New York, a friend of mine saw ahead of him a man whom he felt certain must be English. His clothes were consciously ill-fitting. Hoping that a conversation with this stranger might assuage his homesickness, my friend overtook him and asked the way to Grand Central Station. They began to talk airily of this and that. After a few sentences, a look of suspicion o'erspread the stranger's features.

Stranger: You're a foreigner?

My friend: I'm afraid I'm only English.

Stranger: From London?

My friend: Yes.

Stranger: Do you by any chance know someone called Quentin Crisp?

My friend (positively delighted): I do indeed.

Stranger: I thought somehow you didn't really want to know the way to Grand Central Station.

I once saw a documentary movie in which fishermen cut out the heart of a dogfish and threw it on the deck. There it beat, *diminuendo sostenuto*, for eight hours. This was how, once the war ended, I went on posing in the art schools. During the next three years the zest leaked out of even this occupation which had once represented total fulfilment. There seemed to be no new schools within reach to go to; no new positions to try out that could be held for long enough for students to draw them. I became aware that being a model was a profession at which, after the first year or two, I could not get better. I was bound to get worse. Even the physical agony became monotonous. Boredom, which I now saw was my industrial disease, set in.

I was growing old. My accumulating discontent with posing was really only part of my general state of mind.

It was as though I had been climbing a hill in expectation of finding on the other side a landscape utterly different from the one through which I had passed. Now I was at the summit. I could see that what stretched ahead was exactly the same as what lay behind. For an introvert his environment is himself and can never be subject to startling or unforeseen change. My failures to win true love, to stay in the movie industry, to write books that anyone would publish were not a series of unconnected accidents to which I was prone because of my exposed position in society. They were the expression of my character – the built-in concomitant of a morbid nature to which dreams were more vivid than reality. The infinitesimally small success that I had known had been achieved inevitably in terms of being rather than of doing. I had gained what I had aimed for when I first got control of my own life. But in middle age physical well-being faded. Money, fame, wisdom, which are the booby prizes of the elderly, I had never been able to win. My preoccupation with happiness had been total.

I would not yet have described myself as miserable but I was deflated. I realized that the future was past. Whatever I could hope to do or say or be, I had done and said and been. This state of affairs occurred prematurely because I had subjected a shallow and horribly articulate personality to a lifetime of unflagging scrutiny. Even a marriage with oneself may not last for ever.

Until I was forty it had never dawned on me that I was not immortal. I had once said to the Czech's true love, 'I can never get it into my head that I shall one day die.' She replied, 'Neither can I, but I practise like mad.' I now started to do the same. It was harder for me than for her. Being of a shy and very modest nature, she had been largely content to observe life without disturbing it. My very existence was such that I never had, and never wanted, the opportunity to see people as they would be in my absence. Everything changed the moment I arrived.

While getting on, at differing rates of progress, with our practice, what we both needed was some way of filling in time between now and the grave. She became a Catholic and almost immediately went into a convent.

I took to sex. It became a time filler and ceased to be the pursuit of an ideal.

After about seven years of working in a French prison, the nun returned for one last glimpse of the past. In an upper room in Chelsea, she described to the ballet teacher, the Czech, another of her obsolete true loves and me what her life was now like. She said, 'The trouble with human nature is that you're stuck with it.' She summed up with these words, 'Every hour has been agony but I could not have done otherwise.'

I was finding it much the same with sex except that

for the ennobling influence of anguish I was substituting the degrading effects of discomfort and exhaustion. Sex was not one of my A-level subjects. It is only a mirage, floating in shimmering mockery before the bulging eyes of middle-aged men as they stumble with little whimpers towards the double bed, that somewhere there is a person or a position that will evoke from them sensations of which they dimly dream they are capable. In fact you can only snatch from sex what your nervous system can stand.

In theory, the pursuit of strangers divested of the needless convolutions of romance – the indulgence in chance encounters stripped of the clash of personalities – leads to unfettered self-gratification. In practice it leads rapidly to monotony and, for homosexuals, to danger and expense. Now that I looked so much older, though the treatment I received out of doors was less cruel, indoors I was used much more shoddily. In my own room no one ever actually demanded money with menaces but the hard-luck stories with which I was regaled became shameless. When on one occasion I explained apologetically to someone I had known for fifteen years that at that particular moment I was not able to give him any money, he stole my gold watch. This did not deter him from telephoning me a few weeks later obviously expecting a cosy chat about old times. So much is robbing queers a matter of routine with such men that it was quite a while before he realized that I did not wish to continue our association.

Even if one treasures like pressed flowers these sacred moments of defilement one cannot for long put off the monotony of sex for sex's sake. Staring at the front of people's trousers is, after a time, even less rewarding than gazing into their eyes. As the appeal of any pastime weakens, the habit of it strengthens. I found that it required a continuous effort of will to keep in mind that what was needed to make sex tolerable was not more of it but less.

At least my daylight hours had to be occupied with other thoughts. I had to earn my living and, if I was going to escape from modelling, I would be compelled to return to some kind of employment in which what was left of my brain was used. I went into the art department of a publishing house. This was the first and only job I ever got by answering a newspaper advertisement. I was amazed that my application was successful. So I think were my employers.

I sat at a desk and handled a pen and ink or a brush and poster paint. Except in this, my new occupation was utterly unlike being in any other kind of studio. The pace was that of an Antonioni film; the atmosphere, as undisturbed as a St James's Street club. However lowly your station in life, the treatment you received even from directors was as courteous as a minuet. Doors were held open for you though you were only a speck on the horizon and you were addressed as 'Mr' however angry your interlocutor might be. Most remarkable of all, nobody was ever given the sack. Even had a member of the staff arrived tottering drunk, I am sure he would have been scooped into a taxi, readdressed home and reported to be ill.

Finding it impossible to take any further interest in myself because I had exhausted all the potentialities of my character, I decided, since I was suddenly surrounded by new people in a new setting, that I would try to devote some attention to them. It wasn't easy.

The art editor noticed this. He asked, 'What do you hold with – apart from yourself?' I racked my brains, but I couldn't think of a thing.

The last medium-sized organization that I had worked in had been the film laboratories. There I had seldom been into any other room than the art department and, as I was there only a few months, I never understood the workings of the firm at all. In the publishing house I stayed longer and observed a little more. My first discovery was that, though everybody's feelings were masked by impeccable politeness, each department was slightly afraid of all the others. Quite a lot of time was spent not so much in remedying errors as in disguising them from the scrutiny of neighbours. In the outer world I had been made a fool of for so long and accused of sins so scarlet that admitting to some slight mistake such as having spelt a word incorrectly was like boasting. If anyone had asked me where I felt most at home I could have replied, 'In the wrong.' In the publishing house the pleasures of indiscriminate confession were denied me. I was made conscious that, however unworthily, I was a member of a regiment whose honour was brightened or tarnished by my individual conduct.

The one common bond that united all departments and in moments of danger overcame all uneasiness was the same old hostility towards the ruling caste. When a note was included in everyone's pay packet asking him in future to be more punctual, there was no outcry. That would have been too ungentlemanly. There was a prolonged reverberation of affront. One man uttered the words, 'I wouldn't mind arriving at the right time, if *they* did.' It was difficult to imagine how anyone could hear himself utter a sentence beginning with the words, 'I wouldn't mind arriving at the right time . . .' without laughing, but the complaint was serious. Apparently, even in an organization run like a rest home for retired gentlefolk, the inmates felt themselves to be enduring the humiliations of slavery. To me the job was like going into retreat before facing the rigours of real life again. I luxuriated in my retirement for two and a half years. By that time, by hooligan standards, I was rich. It was my policy never to spend more than half my wages so as not to have to work for more than half my days on earth. At home the drawers where I kept unanswered letters were so full of pound notes that they fell out into the dust whenever I went in search of somebody's address.

When I announced that I was leaving the publishing house, the first words uttered by my immediate boss were, 'You swine.' I think he was chiefly perturbed by the prospect of having to interview new prospective artists. I was hardly a loss to the department. In my room at home I could gladly sit for hours wrapped in a filthy dressing gown and filthier day-dreams about myself, but I became restless when I had nothing to occupy me in other people's time. I was always clamouring for work. The moment I was given anything to do, I couldn't wait to get it finished. The other members of the staff adopted the ruse of filling in the hours by doing the work well. This device never occurred to me. Even when I saw from their example the endless time-consuming possibilities of attention to detail, I could not bring myself to try it. I greatly admired meticulousness, but the capacity for it is part of an entirely different temperament from mine. There are strange people in this world who build galleons in bottles for fun. If I had ever attempted a feat of this nature, before the first spar was in place, I would have been bleeding with knife wounds, sticky with gum and blind with fury.

When the day was fixed for my departure, I received a present from the members of the firm who knew me best. I thanked them with unfeigned amazement. These were the people who had suffered most from the annoyance of having me sitting on the corners of their desks screaming with laughter when I could find nothing better to do. I had been teasingly asked if I intended to go round to every department and shake hands with the entire firm. I had said that I did not but that I would like to see the boss himself before I left. This idea was received with a certain amount of mild mockery. I was still bowing my head before this when a message arrived saying that the boss would like to see me. I wanted to thank him for being so long-suffering. As I stepped into his office, he said, 'I just wanted to say how tolerant I think you've been.'

I left work partly in order not to be doing it and partly because I wanted to write a novel. Until now I had never had the time. I had never been able to collect enough money to live for a year without a job. Now this was possible and at the outset of this period of affluence I was introduced to a publisher who, while we were sitting in what he called 'one of my tatty teashops', suggested that I should write a book. I almost took a taxi home to begin. Six months later I was rushing in the other direction to deliver my typescript to his office.

There are three reasons for becoming a writer. The first is that you need the money; the second, that you have something to say that you think the world should know; and the third is that you can't think what to do with the long winter evenings. I expect the liveliest books are written from a combination of all three motives. I had only the financial one and that may have been part of the cause of my failure. The publisher didn't like the book. .

This was a cause for mourning but hardly for amazement. I am not really equipped to write a novel. As E. M. Forster says, novelists presuppose a world of people interested in human relationships. My trouble was not merely that I was uninterested in them. I didn't think they existed. I tried to write without the literary convention of love and, in the words of one publisher's reader, to succeed in doing this would require genius or at least style. Another comment was that the story was a satire without anger.

I now know that if you describe things as better than they are, you are considered to be romantic; if you describe things as worse than they are, you will be called a realist; and if you describe things exactly as they are, you will be thought of as a satirist. This was the only sense in which my book contained any satire. Every incident depicted had taken place in or on the fringe of my own existence; every line of dialogue had been spoken in my hearing. As there were no sympathetic characters in real life, there were none in my book. Only the pattern of events was invented. If I wrote without anger, this was natural enough for, before an author can write indignantly about the way things are, he must feel that somebody deserved better. The simplest comment on my book came from the ballet teacher. She said, 'I wish you hadn't made every line funny. It's so depressing.'

Of course the most obvious explanation for my total lack of success was that I was a bad writer. This idea I did not entertain for a moment. I continued for months to nag all my friends who had any connection, however slender, with the book racket, into promoting the sale of the book. Finally, when even Fred Urquhart, darting about London with my typescript under his arm, could not produce favourable results, I began to lose interest. There was no actual moment when I decided that further effort was useless. For months the pathetic parcel of greatness continued to lie around in my room waiting to be sent somewhere else. It was removed from the bed at night, from the seat of the armchair during the day, and flung from the desk when there was any drawing to be done. Then the failure of the whole venture became overshadowed by a far greater mistake that at first I did not even know I had made.

Chapter Twenty-five

❦

After being rejected by many religious orders, in some instances because she wasn't rich and in others because she couldn't sing, the Czech's true love finally found a convent that would admit her. She made a request that for some time I had been secretly dreading. She asked me to go occasionally, when she had left the world, to visit the Czech in the mental hospital into which he had been clapped.

About eight times a year for about eight years I made reluctantly the journey that she had undertaken without complaint every Sunday for so long. Added to her special difficulties with travelling was the burden of reproaches with which the patient loaded her for having placed him in captivity. When he was not blaming her, he was demanding that she produce proof that she was herself and not an impostor cunningly got up by *them* to look like her. In spite of the gloomy and sometimes hostile reception that she came to know awaited her, she made this weekly excursion without fail, even in snowy weather which sometimes caused her to fall more than once in a few yards.

When I took over her duty, I was relieved to find I was met with no reproaches and was never asked to prove that I was myself. (Who else could I be?) By that time he had become merely a 'funny old gentleman'. He wore a monocle and decorated his discourse with quaint flourishes of style and quotations from French, Latin and other languages, for he was riddled with Penguin scholarship. He was no trouble. We sat and talked in a room whose floor was so polished that even the sane could hardly stand upright and which was full of inmates and their relatives. We were careful not to look out of the window because among the laurel bushes that luxuriated in the grounds men were in the habit of exposing themselves to the visitors – a sight which tended to interrupt my train of conversation. We drank tea. He purchased three cups explaining, 'The place is an absolute madhouse.'

I tried to perform gladly the chore that had been bequeathed to me but the trouble was that I was stuck with a two-hour journey there, two hours of gibberish and a two-hour journey back in loving mummery of a woman who, being a nun, was as if already dead. The man I was visiting I had never liked even when he was normal. It was distressing to find that, in the midst of his wild mental derangement, his character had remained as unpleasant as before. Even in circumstances where everybody's personality appeared to an outsider to have been reduced to a cypher, he was still snobbish beyond the wildest dreams of the Mitfords, sentimental and oozing with sly, circuitous jokes about sex. However, I was mindful of the fact that soon I too, unless I was very lucky, would reside in an institution which I would doubtless find so boring that even the sight of those who despised me would seem welcome.

Then one day I received from the hospital a letter written partly in Olde Englyshe to warn me that the Czech would be coming to see me. I was surprised, but when I had thought about it, slightly relieved. An outing would constitute a greater diversion for him than a visit in the surroundings that he hated, and I would be spared the long journey out of London and back.

I rejoiced too soon. His arrival was to make greater demands on our thinly spread friendship than I had dreamed possible.

He had hardly been in my room for two minutes before he kissed me. At first I thought that if I remained calm – bordering on benign – what I took to be a squall of sex would subside and serenity would be restored. I was wrong. The situation got worse. It became obvious that this was a climax in our relationship for which the Czech had been waiting for some time. From amazement at the freakishness of this encounter I rapidly passed to the opposite point of view. The whole thing was pathetically inevitable. This was the measure of his loneliness; I was the limit of his degradation. Though I was somewhat confused as to whether or not I was carrying to their logical conclusion the nun's instructions, I felt that I could not do otherwise than try to comply with the wishes of her former lover. If I could not say that I was morally shocked, if I could not claim that I had anything to lose, then it was the least that I could do.

His hair and his whole body were covered with cod-liver oil. He explained that, if, taken internally, it was salubrious, then it must likewise be good for the skin. Also, as I saw for myself, it turned his hair gold. This he felt made him look younger and more desirable. Until this moment it had always puzzled me that fish did not bother with propinquity but, instead, conducted the business of procreation by remote control. I understood them now.

In return for my compliance, though it was less than whole-hearted, the Czech used to bring me tributes of molten chocolate and ruined meat pies which he had somehow obtained from the institution. Once he took the trouble to carry to my room a suitcase full of fallen apples heavy with maggots that spent the afternoon crawling sensually over the bed-cover. At first I tried to act kind of cute on receiving these presents. I said, 'Oh, but you shouldn't have . . .' and I meant it. Even in depravity I lacked stamina and, though his visits thinned out during the course of the ensuing years, my amenability thinned faster. I found myself, at the age of fifty and more, fleeing like a crotchety nymph before a satyr of seventy.

As I look back on this whole episode, I am assailed once again with the feeling that overtakes me whenever I think of anyone that I have known well. I didn't do enough.

Chapter Twenty-six

❧

By the early nineteen fifties, when I was writing my book, the inhabitants of Fitzrovia had come a long way, all of it downhill, from the happy time. Toni had succeeded in offending somebody (and he must have sat up all night to think how to do that) and his clientèle had left in favour of a café called the Alexandria. This place was Toni's mixed with water, as Toni's had been the Low Dive mixed with water.

The Low Dive had set a standard that now only middle-aged hooligans could remember and to which they looked back as Mrs Lot at Sodom. It had been a paperbacked Café Royal, opened, I imagine, especially for outsiders because of its unique location in a dim alleyway in Soho. No sunlight, not even a hated breath of fresh air ever reached its door or those grime-caked gratings that only a house agent could have called windows.

The whole *vie de bohème* was passing without hope or warning. It is a way of life that has two formidable enemies – time and marriage. Even hooligans marry, though they know that marriage is for a little while. It is alimony that is for ever.

There was a shop in Old Compton Street, whose proprietors served tea and coffee with one hand and foreign newspapers with the other. Here I saw the entire cycle from hope to despair acted out before my very eyes in the course of two years. As I sat drinking cup after cup of pale-grey tea some girl that I didn't know from Eve would flop down beside me and engage me in conversation. After a while, with any luck, she would let slip some such words as 'Do you still do Gravesend?' Then I would know that she had been a student there. She would tell me she had won a scholarship to the Slade or the Academy. On her next visit to 'The French' she would be accompanied by a pot-bellied giant with a kitchen-tablecloth shirt and a face that was no more than a clearing in the jungle. After that there seemed only time for another round of teas before she would return with a baby in arms. With it she would sit far back in the café so as not to be questioned about her private life by any policewoman who happened to be passing.

There is no such thing as a hooliganette.

The rest was silence. When next the man was seen it was not in a café but in a public house. He was alone. The girl had been sold into slavery and the child, once hailed as the youngest layabout in the world, was living with its grandparents in Upper Norwood.

This would count as a story with a happy ending. In some cases all souls were lost. The man also went to live in Upper Norwood.

The other enemy of the *vie de bohème* was old age. Hooliganism requires considerable stamina and a degree of adaptability that a lot of people lose with the passing of the years. The monasteries of Bohemia demand more of their brotherhood than some are prepared to give. The daily routine of back-breaking idleness proves too much for certain novices. The self-inflicted orgies that are the inevitable punishment for the slightest deviation into the bourgeois way of life are more than their frail flesh can stand. Many discover to their shame that they have scruples; they have roots and, greatest disadvantage of all, they have hope. The fathers superior of the order do not try to influence their children in Satan; they merely shake their heads in sorrow. They know that the apostate must work out his own damnation.

Even I, though I felt no attraction towards respectability, began to lose some of my enthusiasm for vagabondage. I took a permanent job again in another display outfit. I was introduced to its director by a female inmate of the house where I lived. She was the firm's secretary, though her manner seemed hardly subdued enough for such a position. She was the richest and noisiest girl in the world.

In spite of the fact that she could have bought St James's Palace (and frequently threatened to), as soon as she heard about our house, she longed to live in it. There she felt she would be free.

The place already had the reputation of being a home for incorrigibles. I had taken my room while the landlady was away running a hostel for foreign sailors in Portsmouth where, towards the end of the war, she was almost the only thing left standing. When she came back to London, she accepted me as one of the hazards of her dedication to humanity. Her house was the last in England which was run for the benefit of the tenants. Although this is the age of amateur landladies, some of whom were hooligans in their day, all but my landlady gradually sold out to the other side. They defiled their lips with such phrases as 'Lowering the tone of the neighbourhood' and 'Depreciation of property'. They broke their vows of squalor and changed their role from party-giver to light sleeper.

With the help of time and Mr Wilson I became what Mr Rachman would have called a 'stat', but there is no doubt that I would have been evicted somehow by anyone who was not the patron saint of hooligans.

It was once discovered by the few who went out to work

that there was a strange man sleeping night after night in an armchair stored under the stairs. When they informed my landlady, she was appalled. 'Oh,' she gasped, 'he must be so cold. Couldn't one of you lend him a blanket?'

In these circumstances it required real talent to get turned out, but the display secretary succeeded. In the little back room behind mine, she fought with a boxer dog and its owner until the neighbours ran up the walls and the blood ran down with a gurgling sound. I went permanently into half-mourning when she left. She was a true friend. She used to drive me, squeaking with delight, through the streets of London at eighty-five miles an hour. I was one of her favourite passengers because I was among the happy few who, so far from trying to restrain her rashness, urged her on to greater feats of daring.

As we roared down an avenue of red lights one day, two nuns stepped off the pavement in front of us. 'Get them,' I cried. St Theresa longed to hear the clock strike because every hour was one hour nearer the grave. Since her time there must have been some fresh arrangement. As we swerved towards them, the nuns leapt back on to the path like two huge black crows.

My friend's car was built so that its occupants lay rather than sat with their heads almost on a level with the kerb. It was wide enough for two narrow people but there were often three of us in it. On these occasions I was in the middle partially reclining on the other passenger's fair ripening breast. Every time the driver changed gear she nearly changed my sex. 'You should worry,' she snapped.

The firm of which this girl was, for a while, the secretary was somewhat unconventional. It dealt chiefly in counter display units – stands, trays, containers, which manufacturers employ a special man to cajole or, in the last resort, bully the concessionaires into using in their shops. Everyone hates these labour-creating devices. The travellers are embarrassed at having to distribute them; the retailers resent having to devote time to erecting them. As soon as the manufacturer's man has got back into his car, the shopkeeper flings the display unit into a dim corner of his stock room. The traveller knows this and complains to the board of directors because he knows that what is needed is not a means of bringing the manufacturer's name to public notice but some way of using up excess profits without having to resort to the embarrassing extreme of giving the money to someone who might need it.

The makers of point-of-sale units provide one of the largest and most satisfactory sources of income for the inhabitants of Soho. These gadgets have to be hand-painted and packed. The work can be done at odd times and in odd clothing; it requires no skill and no employment cards. It calls for great concentration of energy for short spaces of time. Squares seem to resent this. Real life, husbands and children make it difficult for them ever to work day and night with only a few hours sleep taken on work benches.

To muster a force of hooligans it is only necessary to know the name of one. Like the inhabitants of the Village of the Damned, information given to one is simultaneously understood by all. The trouble is that outsiders almost never have telephone numbers, often do not have addresses and occasionally do not have names. That I had all three sometimes made me an object of suspicion in Soho.

> Still eyes look coldly upon me;
> Cold voices whisper and say,
> 'He is crazed with the spell of Suburbia.
> They have stolen his wits away . . .'

The monotony of painting display units did not worry me. If I had ever had a soul it had been destroyed long ago. What I expected from any kind of work had changed with the years. I no longer did it to show that I could, as though being employed were a dazzling virtue that I might flaunt before my detractors. I merely wanted a sitting-down job that would yield a change of agony from posing. I was not grieved to find myself engaged in a pursuit that could only lead to more of the same thing. The time for having a career was far behind me.

Without a murmur I painted the faces of four thousand dolls.

Then my boss offered to take me into the firm as a full-time member of her staff of one. I accepted gladly though for me no job could ever be more than a seaside romance with respectability.

My duties as a permanent employee were different from the free-lance work. I made cocoa and washed up the cups; I added up my wages and subtracted my income tax. I typed letters and filed the replies; I answered the telephone and learned how odd my voice sounded to other people. A telephone conversation with an unknown woman client with a baritone voice ended in her saying, 'Your voice is very deep. It's almost as low as mine and I'm frequently taken for a man – over the 'phone, I mean.'

After that, I tried to round out my voice and pitch it lower. I never found a way of eliminating its jangling quality as of a ruined piano that I noticed when I later heard myself speak on a tape-recorder. Almost immediately I began to be offered appointments with fear over the telephone. These were less sinister than the calls I received at home. Receptionists of other firms, who had originally dialled our number in error, rang a second time from a switchboard on which other people were listening.

The only work directly connected with display that I ever attempted was to think up and draw a picture of – or sometimes merely to act out – gimmicks (preferably with some mechanical movement to them). A sub-contractor, once he had understood my mime, could make these in wire or wood or what you will. My far more essential function was to keep the peace between my employer and the outer world. This was no light task. She was never polite to people unless they had more money than she. I pointed out that this behaviour was founded on a vanishing myth. The working classes, whom she thought she was addressing, had long since been replaced by the striking classes.

Strangely enough, to her employee she was extremely kind. As soon as we were alone in the office, which was frequently for days on end, we drank a mixture of Canadian whisky and Coca-Cola and played Scrabble. I played all games seriously – even nastily. They provided an enclosed world whose triumphs compensated me somewhat for a lifetime of defeat elsewhere.

Another interest that we were able to share was watching from the office window the girls leaning against the walls of the street below. We measured the amount of time they were out of sight with the men they had picked up. Including getting into her flat and returning from it to the street, one woman was sometimes away for only seven minutes. In the midst of such preoccupations as these some subcontractor's vanman would appear in the doorway and I would be seized with a spasm of industry. Flinging off my shoes and socks, I would start to run up and down the stairs with boxes under my arm. This activity, which sometimes went on for more than two hours, was so strenuous that I tore my calf muscle from the Achilles tendon. The van was in the street and the office was on the second floor and as many as two hundred and fifty boxes had to be transferred from one to the other before someone came along to tell us that the lorry would have to move on.

When this happened, if the policeman looked inexperienced, I would clasp my hands under my chin and say, 'Oh, officer. Have I done the wrong thing again?' This sometimes had the desired effect. A dazed, almost a bruised look would creep over the face of the young man and he would walk away hardly knowing where he was going.

After four years of these antics I left. If you traffic in ideas on however low a level, four years is a long time. I have yet to meet a commercial artist or a copywriter with a marble clock, but an accountant, if he told you had been with one firm a long time, might mean twenty-four years. It was as well that I left when I did for, about six months after my departure, the firm collapsed. Now the building that housed it has been removed – carefully, like a slice of cake. Weeds grow where once I stood.

While I was still in this display job, I used, after office hours, to pose in evening classes, go to the movies or sit in cafés and pubs. During the past ten years, the ban on me had slowly lifted like a mist. Visibility was now so good in the Coach and Horses that a man was asked to leave because he persistently made fun of me. When this happened I knew for sure that Soho had become a reservation for hooligans. We could at last walk majestically in our natural setting observed but no longer shot at by the safaris that still loved to penetrate this exotic land.

Chapter Twenty-seven

❧

Into the Coach there sometimes came a young woman whom I knew well, but only from having seen her so often in the neighbouring cafés. During a silence that must have been caused by my having to pause for breath, she said, 'Why don't you come and talk to our lot?' Something about this question and in particular about the words 'our lot' warned me that she might be a social worker. I instinctively recoiled, though no opportunity to speak uninterrupted could be allowed to pass without investigation. I began to question her. 'They're raving,' I said and she agreed. It transpired that she spent much of her spare time organizing entertainment for the patients of a day hospital for mental cases. I told her that I would talk to anyone who couldn't get away but that I never spoke for long about anything but myself. 'That wouldn't do,' she said. 'It would be therapeutic.' I thought this objection closed the subject.

A few days later she informed me that she had spoken to the doctors with whom she worked and that they had given permission for me to tell all. So, one Sunday afternoon, weighed down with notes, I went to her hospital and spoke and spoke and spoke.

The snags that I had feared did not crop up. I did not lose my voice and, as we were all sitting cosily in a recreation room and not, as I had feared, in a vast lecture hall, I think I am right in supposing that I could be heard. I found that even 'giving a talk' had its own technique and that I was reading my notes instead of addressing my audience. However, the doctor in charge was polite enough to appear satisfied. He was chiefly glad that what I had said had provoked my hearers to question me and to converse with one another.

The conversation that followed my talk was sad. It was all in psychological terminology. Even patients who had difficulty in arranging their thought in any kind of order at all knew all the long words – all the delusive alibis. This was what always seemed to me wrong with psychology. It did not stop at ridding the misfit of his feeling of shame; it went further and gave him a vocabulary with which to glorify himself. Why should anyone bother whether he steals or not, once he need not say, 'I'm dishonest,' but can claim to be a kleptomaniac?

The final nail was hammered into the coffin of psychology when a friend of mine, whose tears had trickled down to his toes for several weeks, sought the aid of a psychiatrist. He explained his problem and was told that it was nonsense to assert that one man could fall in love with another. All that was needed to set matters right was for my friend to find some nice girl and flop into bed with her. I was interested to know whether this advice was accepted.

Me: Whatever did you do then?

My friend: I rang up Mrs X and she said, 'Very well, dear.'

Me: And are you redeemed?

My friend: It's the same.

Me: Well. Well. Then everything's all right now?

My friend (his tears beginning to flow afresh): It's not. It's more confusing than ever.

A fortnight after my visit to the hospital, I too went to see a psychologist. He had gone to the same institution the following week and been told about my visit. I was surprised that his first question was 'Is there anything you would like to ask me?' He was obviously equally bewildered when I said there was not.

The interview was very short. He told me that he was preparing (yet another) survey of homosexuals and, indeed, of all the minorities he could think of. Twenty years earlier I would have thought this such a noble undertaking. Now I tried not to sigh. As I rose to leave him, the psychologist said in a faintly irritable tone, 'I think it's a pity you dress the way you do but still . . .' I was taken aback by this remark. We seemed to be reading once again that paragraph which used to occur in all books about sexual abnormality and which began, 'There is no need to waste time considering that small group of men who dress and act in an effeminate manner . . .'

Men whose bedroom habits differ markedly from those of their friends have troubles. They touch a spot where no survey can reach but, if these same people feel no compulsion to wear the clothes of the opposite sex or to teeter awkwardly along the vanishing demarcation line between men and women, they have no 'minority' problem whatsoever. In a time outworn, when God was alive and words like 'decency' and 'purity' were used seriously, people objected on moral grounds to associating with men they even suspected of being queer. Now that morality is finished and social convenience is the only criterion of behaviour, it is only obviously effeminate men who are ostracized. It is universally agreed that men are neither heterosexual nor homosexual; they are just sexual.

Of my visit to the day hospital for the insane the ballet teacher asked for what possible purpose it had been arranged. Before I was able to reply, another friend began to say, 'Well, Quentin has a problem of adjusting himself to society and he . . .' This sentence was never finished.

The ballet teacher expostulated, 'I don't agree. Quentin does exactly as he pleases. The rest of us have to adapt ourselves to him.'

This remark seemed to me to outline a great dilemma. Almost all the psychological ills that a man can suffer spring from self-doubt. Once this is removed, his troubles vanish but if anyone really came to believe that he was wise, witty, kind and beautiful, think what troubles his friends would have!

A friend of mine used to come, weighed down with tales of stony-hearted landladies, to the office of the display firm where my boss, temporarily abandoning her rule, fed him with cocoa and allowed him to sleep in her flat on coverlets of leopardette. This was touching, but it was obviously not a permanent solution to his plight. I telephoned a hooligan and his wife who ruled a boarding house in the north of London. They took him in. Thus it became possible to visit my friend and his landlords for the price of one bus fare. Feeling that this was a bargain, I took to going to Crouch End quite often.

One summer's day we were all sitting in a heap in a garden full of broken bicycles and ruined sink baths. My hostess's two children clambered all over her as though she were a playground fixture. Suddenly she declared she couldn't go on living in this way much longer. I had told her, even when she was pregnant, that she had taken the veil for at least seventeen years, with no time off for good conduct. I was distressed to hear her already complaining. Her eldest child was barely three. I asked if she could think of any possible escape route. She said that she needed a huge sum of money. When I questioned her as to how she hoped to come by this, she pointed to a paragraph in one of the culture papers which announced a television play contest.

Once again, and once again fruitlessly as it turned out, I

roused myself. I jumped up and down, swung on the trees, stood on upturned sink baths and declaimed in an all-out effort to bring to life before her very eyes a science-fiction musical ('Take me; make me your flying sorceress') with which I told her that she could easily win any competition. Hitching up her sun suit she rushed indoors and typed a letter to the paper in question to ask for a list of rules for the contest.

When I next visited her, she had received a reply from Granada Television informing her that three plays were required. I ran all the way home and searched under the bed where no human eye had looked for eighteen years and there found two plays, dusty in more senses than one. All the inmates of the Crouch End house were compromised into condensing, retyping and generally warming up these unappetizing left-overs while I searched Soho for a South American guitarist who would write some science-fiction music. The entire combined efforts of all these geniuses were a total loss even though the scripts were accompanied by a covering letter which said, 'Granada shall live again.'

Just as I was sinking uncomfortably back into oblivion, I received a telephone message from the guitarist saying that he had begun yet another musical. I was on the brink of crying, 'Oh, no!' when I realized that I could not fairly do this. If he had so generously written the music for my words, I must now write the words for his music. He explained to me that he wanted a simple boy-meets-girl story with lyrics. This I felt was quite beyond my capabilities. I did not know any boys who met girls. I persuaded him to settle for a 'horror' musical ('Ev'ry little monster wantster'). This play was great fun to write and my association with the composer was without disagreements of any kind. He didn't understand the jokes and I didn't understand the music. I never understood music. It all seemed to me to be the maximum amount of noise conveying the minimum amount of information.

I think of these failures as happy disasters. Unlike the writing of my novel, which took me away from people and used up time in which I could have been speaking, the plays contained built-in success of a small kind. I was able continually to show off before my collaborator. Indeed a large part of our time was spent jumping up and down and exclaiming at each other's greatness. Also failure no longer depressed me deeply. Each unsuccessful attempt to win fame brought me nearer to the time when triumph would be useless even if it came. I had gradually become more or less immune to feeling of every kind and to disappointment in particular. I had been hit in the same place too often. I also had by now learned that the way to deal with unpleasant events was to tell everyone about them. Words had become a salve with which to heal the wounds inflicted on me by experience.

When the war ended and it dawned on me that never again was I likely to play a leading role in the streets of London, I started to live a rich, full life by proxy. I took to the movies. This was an admission of weakness – dearer but less embarrassing than evening classes. All culture – even popular forms of it – was in my eyes a sin. To point out that works of art were beautiful did not justify their creators. Pearls were beautiful but only diseased oysters had them. The enjoyment of works of art seemed to me even more damnable than the fabrication of them, since there could never be any money in it. Moreover, to read a novel or see a play was to drink life through a straw – to smoke it through a filter tip. If we were not afraid of blackening our teeth or riddling our lungs with cancer – if we were a dauntless race of men with strong digestions – we would be able to devour life without the aid of these over-civilized devices.

To minimize my guilt in going to the pictures – to call this wanton pursuit of an effete pleasure by another name – I needed movie companions as drunkards need drinking companions. If I entered a cinema alone, God might plunge his arm through the roof of the auditorium booming in a stereophonic voice, 'And you, Crisp, what are you doing here?' I would never have dared to reply, 'I'm just enjoying myself, Lord.' I remembered too well what happened to Mr and Mrs Adam. A commissionaire with a flaming sword came and asked them to leave. If, however, I could gesticulate towards a friend and shrug my shoulders, I might be thought to have performed an act of self-sacrifice. This would at least divide my shame by two. The trouble was that good movie-goers were hard to come by even though I was willing to pay.

I had just started to feel the pull of the expanding universe. The life that starts in the heart of London gradually drifts outward. As my friends became older, many of them married and moved out of Soho into the suburbs where their failure would be less apparent. If their unions were cursed and children were born to them, they went even farther. By the time I was forty-five, I found that almost all my older friends had gone, if not like Henry Vaughan's into a world of light, at least on to the North Circular Road. I had to nag strangers into coming to the cinema with me. This was hard work, for the strangers who were willing to talk to me in cafés were hooligans and hooligans do not like entertainment. They will talk and they will drink, in their weaker moments they will even eat, but they will not go to a theatre or read a book or see a film.

Even so I managed to go to the pictures – and never alone – on an average once a week for many years; sometimes I went three times in three consecutive days and, very occasionally, twice in one day, thus spending seven hours out of twenty-four in the 'forgetting chamber'. Real life became for me like a series of those jarring moments when the screen goes blinding white, the jagged edge of a torn strip of film flicks one's eye-balls and there is a flash of incomprehensible numerals lying on their sides (like a message in code from Hades) before the dream begins again.

I gladly saw almost any film unless it was English. My taste in movies had changed very little since the far-off days when, in the Black Cat, I and my friends had acted out to each other the stories of the various pictures we had seen. I was still a devotee of the divine woman.

In my lifetime she changed her name three times, calling herself first Brigitte Helm, later Greta Garbo and finally Marlene Dietrich. I thought about her a great deal, wore her clothes, said her sphinx-like lines and ruled her kingdom. I came to the conclusion that beauty was not a girl but an Aryan face seen through Semitic eyes. This was what gave her that tragic and remote quality. If what the Wandering Jew (who might by now have changed his name to Fritz Lang) most longed for was unbearable pleasure indefinitely prolonged, then he had to invent for himself a woman who was both beautiful and unattainable.

We have come a long degrading way from Miss Helm to Mlle Bardot. The fault lies not in our movie stars but in ourselves. Those beauties of the last generation symbolized hopeless love. Now it is too late for tears. What modern young man has the time to play a guitar under his true love's window or the energy to climb up the ivy into her room? In bed he is embracing the bomb. Someone had to invent espresso sex and to serve each cup of this tasteless beverage there had to be a mechanical doll whose only recommendation was her infinite availability. The woman who came to embody this ideal to the full

207

was Marilyn Monroe. Her directors persuaded her to flaunt her astonishing sexual equipment before us with the touching defencelessness of a retarded child. She was what the modern young man most desires in life – a mistress who could be won without being wooed. She was the football pool of love.

This was no kind of diet for anyone brought up on Rider Haggard. Nevertheless, I continued to linger in the one-and-ninepennies on the principle that any film is at least better than real life. In the absence of stars, I began to concentrate on the stories. I became disturbed by their curious morality. It seemed that to script-writers sex was sacred and money was damned. Over and over again I saw heroines forgiven – even praised – for the most dubious behaviour if they could claim that their object had been sexual fulfilment. To me this seemed not merely a flimsy excuse but a circumstance that only increased the crime. My views on this subject were expressed once and for all by a char hired by a friend of mine. She was unaware that she had begun to live in a street of shame. The cleaner knew not only what sins were committed but who was committing them and her comments were an education to my friend. The most enlightening day of all was when the char dragged her by the sleeve to the front window and said of a figure disappearing round the corner of the street, 'Quick, madam. Look at that one. Girls that do it for money are bad enough but *she* does it to oblige.' This was a moral standpoint that no film-maker would ever have understood.

When movie ethics became too confusing for me I ceased to bother about them and turned my attention to the technique of film construction. Before long, even this interest was snatched from me by the modern passion for the haphazard – for the abandonment of style. When

Antonioni ascended the celluloid throne, pictures became as boring as being alive.

After almost twenty years in the twilit zone, I came blinking back into the light of day.

Chapter Twenty-eight

❧

I would never have embarked even upon such a cosy disaster as writing a 'horror' musical, if the opportunity had not presented itself when I had nothing profitable to do. I left the display job in November and there was just time to write *Carry On, Hearse!* or *The Thing and I* before the start of what the schools mockingly call 'Spring' term. I was going back to posing not because I still preferred it to all other ways of earning a living but because there was nothing else for me to do.

Only four years had gone by since I had last been a full-time model, but I was shocked to find how much worse the situation had become. During the war things had been somewhat haphazard. Now students enrolled for chaos. Work had almost ceased. The young people wandered through the corridors in droves, shouting, cursing, singing, necking.

The amount of life drawing available to them had increased, but their interest in it dwindled and had in some cases vanished altogether. Although these young people took almost no notice whatsoever of what went on in the outer world, they did go to the galleries and in them they no longer saw any paintings of naked girls flopping about on piles of cushions. No nudes was good news. This change in aesthetic fashion meant that they could produce a large number of pictures with very little study. The sudden arrival of a model in the life room signified a temporary return to a pursuit that was old-fashioned, unprofitable and difficult.

One art school in Kent was, I felt, a kind of cultural Borstal. While working there, out of the corner of my eye I perceived two students lying one on top of the other on a long wooden box which had been pushed into a corner of the life room. The art master saw the look of horror that o'erspread my withered features and followed the line of my gaze to its cause. Standing over the entangled couple, he waited, thinking that the very proximity of so much contempt would chill their ardour. This proved a vain hope. He was compelled to stoop and, plunging his hand into the matted hair of the girl, to prise her face from that of her lover. There was a sound like tearing sticking plaster from a painful wound. I thought the young man would say, 'The woman thou gavest me, tempted me . . .' but no! From eyes dull with debauchery, sunk in faces glistening with saliva, the two pupils gave their teacher a sullen stare. Then, very slowly, they got up and returned to their easels.

If being treated with indifference was now the daily lot of most models, it was obvious that open contempt would be shown to me. I was a natural target and my heroic postures on the throne now seemed more ludicrously out-moded than ever. In some schools the mounting hostility led to insults about my appearance and my private life being hurled at me by students sitting on the window ledges to watch me arrive and depart.

I found it depressing that this kind of behaviour should still prevail. On so many levels, the age of tolerance was in full bloom. The Utopia, dreamed of by me and the friends of my youth, was here. Anyone could do or say or wear anything without being arrested – almost without public disapproval. This applied particularly to men's wear about which, when I was young, everyone had been so sensitive. A factor no one had foreseen had come to the aid of the party. The population of England now contained more men than women. Therefore masculine plumage had become more colourful. Also Mr Bronowski's arrow of time, which, he assures us, always points in the direction of diminishing difference, had struck at the heart of our civilization. The distinction between the sexes was reduced to the point where it would have been difficult to tell the boys from the girls if the clothes of the young men had not become so sexually revealing. Indeed their trousers could go no further – or, should it be, no nearer – unless they adopted a Plantagenet style, wore tights and carried their pride and joy in a specially tailored sack tied with two smart bows.

All these strange manifestations do not prove that more copulation is going on in the world than formerly but that sex, as an idea – as a topic of conversation – is enjoying a freedom never before known and what can be spoken of soon comes to be condoned. If you asked the man in the modern street for his opinion of homosexuality, he would probably reply, 'I've nothing against queers myself but I wouldn't like one of them to marry my father.'

In Neuilly-sur-Seine there is an apartment house in the hall of which this notice is pinned up: 'In this establishment window-boxes are strictly forbidden. Will each tenant therefore make sure that his are firmly fixed to the window-sills.' It is odd that this admonition should have been issued in France. It seems to typify a particularly English mode of thought and one that currently applies to the national attitude towards homosexuality. The law remained the same as it was before Brigid Brophy was born, but public opinion had moved on. This 'window-box' morality was offensive to legalists and logicians, but to homosexuals it was easily acceptable. As a member of the Law Reform Society said, in tones trembling with reproach, 'It's you – the people concerned – that are so hopelessly indifferent.' This is true. The fundamental predicament of homosexuals is one that no amount of legislation can improve. Even the argument that the repeal of the laws against private indecency will lessen opportunities for blackmail is founded on a misunderstanding. No one in his right senses will attempt to blackmail anyone to the police. The realization of the threat would merely lead to both parties being clapped into a dungeon. Blackmail operates by the threat to reveal facts of which a man is ashamed to those whose good opinion he prizes. This is hardly ever likely to be the C.I.D. It may easily be the victim's mother or wife or employer. To rob blackmail of its potency, it would be necessary to remove the homosexual's feeling of shame. This no power on earth can do. From this feeling of inadequacy and exile I was not immune. The only difference between me and other outsiders was that I cried aloud for pardon. Almost every living being seems to feel that if all were known he would be admired and even I was never able to rid myself of the idea that if all were known I would be forgiven.

At least a step in this direction was taken when it was at last understood that human beings respond to almost any erotic stimulus. It was only while people still felt that God was watching them that they directed their impulses exclusively towards certain parts of certain people. In everybody the anus is at least as capable of sexual excitement as the lips. Sex acts are now termed masculine and others feminine only to keep the subject tidy.

In my own life a mystery still lingers. It seems that, as a child, I was particularly susceptible to anal stimulus and that my repeated 'accidents' were the result of my unwillingness to forgo the pleasure of retaining my faeces until it was too late. It would be unreasonable to think that at that age I deliberately adopted an effeminate exterior in the hope that this would one day introduce me to other ways of obtaining the same satisfaction. On the other hand, it is difficult not to presume some connection.

All the intimate subjects which were now being discussed so loudly in such public places had been known on higher levels for a long time, but the knowledge had only recently seeped down to places where it made a difference to the general attitude toward kinkiness. As Brophy's First Law says, it is not the simple statement of facts that ushers in freedom; it is the constant repetition of them that has this liberating effect. Tolerance is the result not of enlightenment, but of boredom.

The sad truth remains, however, that adolescents must have something to scorn at least as much as they feel themselves to be scorned. 'Queer-baiting' has not vanished. It has fallen into the hands of younger and younger boys. Quite recently I was asked for money and, when I feigned not to have heard, was kicked in the groin and threatened with worse by six children young enough to demand half fares when they scrambled on to the bus that I had boarded to escape them. This incident was not a boyish prank. The leaders of the gang knew all the wounding words and were sufficiently worldly to threaten to tell the police that I had tampered with them in Trafalgar Square.

If all the praise that I had ever received seemed no more than my due, it follows that all the rough treatment that I underwent appeared undeserved. Only by a great effort at detachment could I see that to other people my appearance, which had once provoked them to indignation because it represented sin, now aggravated them because it had become the overemphatic statement of a tired axiom. To the younger generation to whom the words 'good and evil', 'innocence and guilt' have lost all meaning, it was no longer my wickedness that annoyed them; it was my pomposity – my insistence on taking the blame for something on which judgment was no longer passed. Also, by an unlucky chance, the symbols which I had adopted forty years earlier to express my sexual type had become the uniform of all young people. By wearing bright colours and growing my hair long I had by mistake become the oldest teenager in the business. It was irritating for the men to see me converting their attire to my own ends. I inadvertently gave the impression of trying to gate-crash a King's Road party for people two generations younger than I. I was not merely a stopped clock; I was a stopped grandfather clock. Before this criticism I was defenceless. It was much too late for me to rejoin the human race I had left in childhood. I would have had no idea how to go on in the presence of real people as their equal. If I had originally been a member of their club, I had certainly never paid my dues and, as Macbeth would have said, 'I was in tinsel stepped in so far that, should I wade no more, returning were as tedious as go o'er.'

Chapter Twenty-nine

❧

For the first three years after I returned to posing I did not take any of the drawbacks involved very seriously. I expected them – indeed, the whole world – to end at any moment.

When the war threw me over, I took up with the atom bomb. We were to be married in the spring of 1963. Take heart, I said to myself, all may yet be lost. *Time* magazine, which cannot be contradicted except by its own subsequent issues, promised that something called the 'missile gap' would then be at its widest. They said that when this happened, the enemy would strike. They and I were unduly optimistic.

That was years ago. If the bomb comes now it will be too late. I shall embrace radio-activity only in the resigned spirit in which Laetitia agreed to marry the Egoist – partly to round off the story and partly to save the bomb's good name.

Recently I have inclined towards the view that there should not be this undignified element of hazard about the date of a person's demise. There ought to be a Ministry of Death, though, in Orwellian terminology, it would be named the Ministry of Heaven. This august body of men, all preferably under thirty years of age, would deal with the chore of exterminating old people. Before everything else they would have to agree upon a time limit (say, sixty) to live beyond which would be an offence (punishable with life?). Then the ministry would have to make sure that, six months before his sixtieth birthday, every living being received a notice offering post-dated congratulations and advising him which town hall he would be required to visit on the happy occasion. A week before his birthday he would receive a final notice and then, at the glorious hour, unless he preferred to walk there on his own two feet, the van would call to take him to oblivion. In America this vehicle would be painted to look like a fiery chariot but in England it would be plain blue with the words 'Ministry of Death, Kensington Branch' discreetly lettered on its side. For the first few years after such a law was passed there might occasionally be undignified scenes, but in Britain individual liberty is so often curtailed for the common good. Order would soon prevail. Everyone would come to see that the idea was basically good. It would eliminate the dreary effort put by most middle-aged people into trying to set up circumstances conducive to a tolerable old age which, in many cases, never comes. Above all, the creation of this new government body would end the racially suicidal practice of limiting the number of young people in the world by the use of contraceptives. It would substitute a decrease in the heaps of old men and women cluttering up the planet. To this law there would be no exception on grounds of lack of hardship and no extensions of time, but some people might wish to avail themselves of the ministry's services at an earlier date than that prescribed. They would be allowed to make two applications, separated in time by an interval of at least six months, so that the authorities might review their financial status and make sure that public facilities were not being used for the purpose of avoiding payment of private debts. This would also permit applicants to change their mind if their first application had been made in a fine, careless anguish.

Like any other new political measure, the Laws of

Death would come trailing crowds of snoopers, fixers and black marketeers peddling contraband old age at exorbitant prices; if food rationing worked in spite of the inhuman element, so would the controlled apportioning of days.

If the government does not soon adopt some such plan as I have outlined, I shall have to put into action a more personal scheme for limiting my span of years. I shall commit a murder. This is something that for a long time I have wanted to do. It is a natural extension of the desire to hit strangers in the street or to answer them back. It would have been impossible to get through the kind of life that I have known without accumulating a vast unused stockpile of rage. Retaliation, though, was a luxury I could never afford. On the physical level I was too feeble. On any other I was not rich enough. I never dared be rude to anyone. I never knew that I might not need him later. Long after fantasies of sexual excess had ceased to torment me, my imagination was inflamed by lurid day-dreams of having my revenge on the world. Whenever people read in the papers that someone has purchased a machine-gun and mowed down a whole neighbourhood, they invariably say, 'I wonder what brought that on.' They even make some such remark when the subject is an American Negro. To me the motive is self-evident. Mass-murderers are simply people who have had ENOUGH.

Wishing to go out in a blaze of ignominy, I shall limit my activities to killing a policeman. If I am not arrested for the first murder, I shall try a second. It will be like a game of musical chairs.

In the meantime I continued to pose in the art schools – chiefly in the recreational classes. As I sank into old age I was more often given portrait sittings. This was not because my face had crumbled any less than my figure. It was in an even worse state of repair. My teeth became such that my dentist said, 'It's not your teeth that are decaying. It's you.' As my character coarsened, my features thickened. On the other hand my hair thinned. A receding hair line can be thought to add to the face an undeserved look of nobility but when you are noble all the way to the crown of your head, you're in trouble. However, certain Slade-type students can paint a tragic greatness into eyes that hang like an impending avalanche over the cheekbones. Nothing for which the life beautiful has a name can be read into a pot-belly.

Professionally it is considered a come-down to work in portrait classes, but at least head sittings were less exacting than other kinds. I did them with what grace and gratitude I could. My lust for martyrdom had vanished long ago.

I had never been legally married to real life. Between the ages of twenty-two and forty I had merely conducted an uneasy and illicit liaison with it. In taking up modelling once more, it transpired that I had gone home to mother culture once too often. I made a desperate effort to get another full-time job but now, not only my odd appearance, but also my age were against me. All doors were shut. I fell back into the oubliette of art. In its Havisham twilight I was grimly at home. About me there was something of the dusty elaboration of her mouse-nibbled wedding cake. So here, propped up on some rickety Victorian chair, I sat silent and, I hope, apparently resigned – an ashy clinker from the long dead fires of Bohemia . . .

Ironically, long after the shouting and the tumult had died, a feature-writer from the London office of the *Scotsman* telephoned. He suggested that he should write an article about me. I agreed and a very urbane gentleman with no kilt and no accent came to question me. 'They've got the idea that you're the most famous model in the world – up there,' he said.

Me: In heaven?

Scotsman: No. In Edinburgh.

Me: Pity.

Scotsman: Is there any justification for this opinion?

Sadly I explained that, as far as I knew, the conditions in which anyone could be a famous model had vanished long ago. Those few of us who were still in the racket had dwindled into naked Civil Servants.

What happened? What went wrong?

This is the question that, from a throat parched by brick dust, I ask the rescue party as they lean for a moment's rest on their Reform Bills and their Acts of Parliament. When they see me tottering towards them, they find it difficult not to recoil. I am the survivor they hoped they would not find – something too broken to be restored to active life but not quite ready for decent burial. My lips still move.

I have learned, though I never mastered it, the modern manner. I know that on no account must I point a moral or trace a pattern through my past. I clearly see that my life was only an imprudent dash between the cradle and the tomb across open country and under fire. Yet I find it hard to take a prolonged look back and not attempt to excuse results by rearranging causes. Though intelligence is powerless to modify character, it is a dab hand at finding euphemisms for its weaknesses. D. H. Lawrence said that it was not living life that mattered but watching it being lived. I would say that it was not watching life that mattered but explaining what you saw.

Some years ago, in a New York house, the windows of which were never opened, two brothers lived. One of them became blind and partially paralysed. Towards the end of his life he never went out at all; the other left the house briefly to buy food and newspapers with which, after a while, the rooms were piled so high that the place was transformed into a network of canyons from one strategic point to another. To keep out intruders every inch of this labyrinth was mined with booby traps. One day one of these was set off by accident. When, months later, the corpses of the brothers were found, one of them was still sitting up in bed waiting for the other. The second lay only a few yards away pinned by tons of newsprint to the floor. Even before he was quite dead, the rats had begun to gnaw at his body.

In a sense this was the way I lived, this the fate that overtook me. The place where no harm can come is the place where nothing at all can come. Here I stood. By constituting myself the one among the many I had provoked the worst behaviour in others. With this I felt compelled to deal politely. This wrought no change whatever in the character of my enemies but caused the total disintegration of my own. In the end the habit of taking no notice diminished my perception to the point where I became impervious to influence of any kind and therefore to all change except decay. I grew boring to my friends and, which was worse, to myself. I wanted nothing except to get into my coffin without getting into debt.

But, when I ask myself what went wrong, what do I feel that I missed?

Love?

No one has ever been in love with me even faintly – even for half an hour, or if they have, it was a well-kept secret. Yet I can write this sentence with nothing more than a feeling of wounded vanity. I experience no keen sense of loss because I, myself, was never in love with anyone and do not clearly know what the expression means.

Fame?

If fame is merely to be known by a large number of people whom one does not oneself know, then I was famous or at least notorious for many years. The most that I can say is that some by-products of this state of affairs were amusing.

Power was what I craved most ravenously, though not because I felt I merited it. If I had had what I deserved in life I would have starved long ago. I wanted dominion over others in order to redress the balance. A lifetime of being constantly at the mercy of others left me, even though mercy was undoubtedly shown, crushed and seething with a lust for tyranny. No one forced me into the role of a victim. Indeed many of my friends tried to lead me out of it, but the wall-to-wall puritanism of my early years made me excruciatingly conscious of the 'sin' of homosexuality. I had no alternative use for my passion for showy extremes but to make with it a Carnaby Street hair-shirt.

All this at the last I dimly saw, but an autobiography is an obituary in serial form with the last instalment missing. We think we write definitively of those parts of our nature that are dead and therefore beyond change, but that which writes is still changing – still in doubt. Even a monotonously undeviating path of self-examination does not necessarily lead to a mountain of self-knowledge. I stumble towards my grave confused and hurt and hungry . . .

P.S.

Ideas,
interviews
& features . . .

About the author

Read on

Naked Civil Rights: the fall and rise of homosexual freedoms

by Louise Tucker

'"Gay" history will, as time goes by, evaporate. As it becomes unimportant what sex people have, we shall only be a tiny footnote in the dictionary of the world.' Quentin Crisp

QUENTIN CRISP DESCRIBED his autobiography as 'an obituary in serial form with the last instalment missing'. Its publication changed the course of that last instalment in ways that, when commissioned, he doubtless never expected, bringing him the sort of fame that he had once fantasized about yet accepted he would never attain. Published in 1968, only a year after the repeal of the Buggery Act of 1533, the book was not an instant success. In fact, as Crisp himself points out, it was television that made it, and him, into a legend:

> Looking back, the press likes to refer to the book as 'a bestseller at the time'. It was no such thing. It received respectful reviews, sold about 3,500 copies, and caused no sensation whatsoever until it was translated into a television scenario by Mr. Mackie . . . [he] cajoled Thames Television into making his script into a television play . . . *The Naked Civil Servant* was well received – even by critics. Their approbation caused awards to be sprinkled like confetti upon Mr. John Hurt, who played the leading part in it, on

its director, Mr. Gold, on its production team, headed by Miss Lambert, and on Mr. Mackie. No credit for the excellence of this play is due to Mr. Crisp; he is merely the raw material from which it is made. (Source: The Quentin Crisp Archives, www.crisperanto.com)

But television, as ever, could turn a nobody into a somebody and thanks to the play's success in 1975 Crisp became a personality, famous simply for being himself. A lifetime of posing had, at the age of 67, paid off. Six years later he moved to New York where for the next two decades he enjoyed, as a pensioner, the sort of career that he had, in his twenties, considered out of reach. In some senses, he had become what he would have described as 'a senile delinquent': he appeared in films (notably Sally Potter's *Orlando* as Elizabeth I in 1992, aged 84), wrote books and reviews and starred in his own one-man show, *An Evening with Quentin Crisp*. Having fallen in love with North America, especially with New York, it was ironic that he should die in England, in Manchester, on the night before another tour of his show. He was 90.

Both in the last years of his life, and since his death, Crisp has frequently been described as the twentieth century's Oscar Wilde or Wilde's 'perfect descendant' and in many respects the two men were similar. Writers, dandies and satirists, both refused to curtain or curtail their sexuality in a ▶

BORN:
Christmas Day 1908, Surrey

LIVED:
London and New York

CAREER:
Artist's model, graphic designer and commercial artist, writer, public speaker

DIED:
1999, Manchester

3

Naked Civil Rights: the fall and rise of homosexual freedoms *(continued)*

◀ society that outlawed it. Only sixty years separates them, and yet Crisp's later life, and death, were very different from his predecessor's. Wilde, born in 1854, could have been Crisp's grandfather, or even father, but the societies into which they were born and lived bore no resemblance to each other. Whereas Crisp escaped legal if not social censure in the early twentieth century, the nineteenth century was not so lenient and Wilde was imprisoned for 'gross indecency' in 1895. Whereas Wilde's life was both cut short and ruined by his conviction for homosexuality, Crisp was feted and lauded for his book revealing the life of a gay man. Whereas Wilde's life ended in 1900 in ignominy in Paris, Crisp's ended at the peak of his success almost a hundred years later. For Crisp, unlike Wilde, it was easy, eventually, to be out and gay. 'Tolerance,' he wrote, 'is the result not of enlightenment, but of boredom.' It would seem then that the world has changed immeasurably since Wilde's death: homosexuality is mainstream, gay rights no longer need to be fought for and, as Crisp himself pointed out, the police officers in Soho, London, may have questioned his practices but those on Second Avenue asked after his performances.

But has it changed so much? As I write this, in England in 2006, I know that it is relatively obvious that no self-respecting metropolitan media organization, whether a television station, marketing company or publishing house, is going to make a fuss about an employee's sexuality. But I'm not so

❛ Crisp has frequently been described as the twentieth century's Oscar Wilde or Wilde's "perfect descendant" ❜

sure about a factory, a supermarket or an insurance office in the provinces. Television in particular has the effect of neutralizing difference, enshrining it in a personality so that it's OK to laugh openly at Graham, Julian and Rupert on talk shows, even if the laughter about Gordon in the accounts department isn't quite so innocent. Crisp himself pointed out that appearing on television had saved him from negative reactions: 'if you discuss it on television, it is perfectly all right. You can murder your mother and it is acceptable if you are a guest on an American TV talk show.'

Money, fame and status can defuse and deflect criticism of what would, for some in other circumstances, be unacceptable behaviour. At least they can in New York, Paris and Berlin; in other parts of the world, interestingly many of them former English colonies, being gay is still a death sentence, whatever your position. A few months after Britain and Canada made civil unions and same-sex marriage part of legal statute, the *Sunday Herald* newspaper in Jamaica ran the following headline: 'No homos'. In the paper Bruce Golding, the leader of the opposition and the Jamaica Labour Party, stated that 'homosexuals would find no solace in any cabinet formed by him'. He was supported by members of the clergy and a trade union leader. In Jamaica sex between men is illegal, whether in public or private, and punishable with up to ten years in jail, and throughout the English-speaking Caribbean being openly homosexual is impossible. ▶

6 "Tolerance is the result not of enlightenment, but of boredom." 9

*Other autobiographies by
Quentin Crisp*

How to Become a Virgin
and *Resident Alien: The
New York Diaries*
Crisp's second volume of
autobiography continues
his life story,
post-publication of his
first book and its
dramatization; in
his third he turns his
wit and gaze on New
York, his home for the
last decades of his life.

Naked Civil Rights: the fall and rise of homosexual freedoms *(continued)*

◄ Christian values are frequently cited as the reason for this, but that does not explain why many reggae artists, not usually renowned for their religious fervour, suggest burning and killing gay men in their lyrics.

In fact, Jamaica, and most of the English-speaking Caribbean, can thank King Henry VIII and the Buggery Act of 1533 for their legal statute banning homosexuality. The king made buggery punishable by hanging, a penalty only lifted in 1861 (six years after the birth of Oscar Wilde), and the act affected the whole English-speaking world both then and now. Though England and Wales repealed all such laws in 1967 (Scotland and Northern Ireland waited till 1979 and 1982 respectively), a year before the publication of *The Naked Civil Servant*, legal statutes in many former colonies kept them. Like the abortion debate in the US, homosexuality is a powerful political motivator in Jamaica, and political parties have no interest in repealing the sodomy laws, despite calls from the European Parliament to do so. Thus five hundred years after the law became statute, gay men and women are still fleeing the island for their lives. J-FLAG, the Jamaica Forum for Lesbians, All-Sexuals and Gays, reported that they know of 30 gay men who have been murdered in Jamaica between 1997 and 2004. (Source: *Guardian*, 'If You're Gay in Jamaica, You're Dead', by Diane Taylor, 2 August 2004.)

Perhaps in countries where religious belief is paramount, such intolerance is to be expected. It seems unsurprising, for those in the West, that in Iran and Saudi Arabia anyone suspected and/or convicted of homosexual acts will be executed. And yet such binary divides between East/West, religious/irreligious, intolerant/tolerant, uncivilized/civilized cannot be maintained and nowhere is this more obvious in a country that would position itself at the other end of the spectrum to the Middle East: the United States.

Home of one of the first gay rights organizations, renowned for promoting sexual and racial equality, the US has always liked to consider itself a world leader in stamping out discrimination. At least it has federally but the US is much more of a continent than a country, and its citizens, like drinking laws and banking practices, are often divided from each other along state lines. Nowhere is this more obvious than in the debate on gay marriage. Whereas in Massachusetts, marriage for same-sex partnerships is legal, only five other states currently offer civil unions or domestic partnerships. The issue is wonderfully confused by the fact that across the border in Canada, same-sex marriages are legal throughout the country . . . and the US and its neighbour have a history of respecting marriages contracted in either jurisdiction. Couples from North Dakota can therefore be married across the border in Manitoba, and come back, at least in theory, as a legally accepted married couple. Social acceptance of homosexuality in the States is also no more established than the required laws. ▶

FIND OUT MORE

www.crisperanto.org
The Quentin Crisp archives are incredibly detailed and include interviews, biographies, early photos of Crisp as an artist's model as well as snippets of choice information from those who knew him.

Orlando (director: Sally Potter)
Quentin Crisp played the decrepit and powdery Elizabeth I in this fantastically over the top yet relatively faithful film of Virginia Woolf's gender-critical novel.

The Naked Civil Servant
John Hurt plays Crisp and was much praised for his performance. During the filming the actor and his character discovered that one (Hurt) had painted the other when he was an art student.

Philadelphia
Quentin Crisp appears as a guest at a party in this 1993 film about homophobia in the United States.

Naked Civil Rights: the fall and rise of homosexual freedoms (*continued*)

◀ So although episodes of a sitcom such as *Will and Grace* suggest that every American is happy to have a gay best friend, headlines detailing how Matthew Shepard was beaten to death, in Wyoming, by two homophobic thieves rather contradict that impression. There may not be public executions in the US – like that of two young men suspected of homosexuality in Iran in 2005 – but the death of Shepard, tied to a fence and beaten to a pulp, suggests that there are still private ones.

The best place to be gay, in legal terms, is not, and has never been, the US; it has almost always been Scandinavia. In the eleventh century only sons who inherited their fathers' land could marry; the others had to leave the family home and join warrior societies. Since women at this period were expected to remain chaste, unavailable and untouchable, the men in these societies turned to each other, and pederasty, relationships between older and younger men, was institutionalized as a result. Throughout the twentieth century the Netherlands and Scandinavia continued to be trailblazers, putting the rest of Europe in the shade in terms of progress. Sweden was the first to decriminalize homosexuality in 1944, the first to pass anti-discrimination laws with respect to taxes, inheritances and social services in 1988 and the first to allow same-sex adoption laws in 2002 . . . no wonder ABBA are such gay icons. Denmark was the first country to enact civil union laws in 1989, and the first and still extant gay liberation organization was formed in Holland in 1946.

But even amongst the good news, the forward-thinking establishment of civil unions and domestic partnerships, there is always bad news: New Zealand has made civil unions possible but its near-neighbour Australia refuses to consider them. And 'twas ever thus'. It is little known for example that when concentration camps were liberated in 1945, all homosexual prisoners, convicted by the Nazis under Germany's notorious Paragraph 175, were not released, nor were their original convictions, however spurious, quashed.

In some respects the world in which Quentin Crisp died is very different from the one in which he was born. And perhaps his bravery at being himself made a difference. However, what has not changed, and may never change, is the sense that a public figure can in many countries be openly gay without fear of censure, but in private life it is not so simple. Money and fame are often useful distractions for those who might otherwise discriminate. Even fifteen years after the death of one of the most publicly accepted gay men, there is nothing naked about the lives of most gay people. Their civil rights and lives are often still veiled.

(Sources: www.crisperanto.org;
http://en.wikipedia.org/wiki/1929_in_gay_rights;
http://en.wikipedia.org/wiki/LGBT_rights_in_Jamaica.
Accessed 6 October 2006.) ■

◀ doesn't seem very likely, it will be very poorly lit and full of people they can feel pretty confident they will never meet again.'

'When I returned to the States after completing *Orlando*, I was stopped by the passport officer because of my status as a resident alien. He was an enormous man with a shaved head – he looked like an absolute thug. I thought, "Poor me, my time has come!" And then the officer leaned over the barrier, pressed the passport back into my hand and whispered, "It must feel good to be so utterly vindicated." And it does.' (Source: 'An Englishman in New York', Chris Mitchell, *Spike*, www.spikemagazine.com/spikejun.php; accessed 2 October 2006.) ■

If You Liked This, Why Not Try More from the *Stranger Than* series . . .

Wild Swans
Jung Chang
Breathtaking in its scope, unforgettable in its descriptions, this is a masterpiece which is extraordinary in every way.

Through the story of three generations of women in her own family – the grandmother given to the warlord as a concubine, the Communist elite mother, the disgraced daughter – Jung Chang reveals the epic history of China's twentieth century.

Few books have had such an impact as *Wild Swans*: a popular bestseller which has sold more than 10 million copies and a critically acclaimed history; a tragic tale of nightmarish cruelty and an uplifting story of bravery and survival.

'Riveting, an extraordinary epic'
Mail on Sunday

Angela's Ashes
Frank McCourt
Before the film, before the Pulitzer Prize, before the international acclaim, there was a book. The memoir of a New York schoolteacher's poverty-stricken childhood in Limerick, the energy, wit, passion and sheer power of the story caught the imagination and captured the hearts of those who read it – and they then told everyone they knew to read it too.

A story that has moved millions; a classic of modern autobiography; a tale too human, too captivating not to be read.

'It sings with irreverent wit'   *The Times*

Longitude
Dava Sobel

The dramatic human story of an epic scientific quest, *Longitude* is a phenomenon, an international bestseller so successful that it launched a whole new wave of writing.

The 'longitude problem' was the thorniest dilemma of the eighteenth century: without the ability to measure it sailors throughout the ages had been literally lost at sea. With £20,000 at stake, it became a web of political intrigue and intellectual brilliance, of personal ambition and foul play. And at its very heart stood John Harrison, a self-taught Yorkshire clockmaker, who battled the establishment in his quest to make the perfect timekeeper and scoop the spoils.

'A true-life thriller, jam-packed with political intrigue, international warfare, personal feuds and financial skullduggery'
FRANCIS WHEEN, *Daily Mail*

If You Liked This . . .
(continued)

The Perfect Storm
Sebastian Junger

It was a 'perfect' storm – perfect, meteorologically, in that it could not be worse. It found its terrible heart 500 miles off the coast of Massachusetts, coming to fruition in 120-mile-an-hour winds and ten-storey waves. And into its path wandered the fishing boat *Andrea Gail* and her six-man crew.

To be an international bestseller for over four years a story must be an epic, told by a master storyteller. Terrifying, sad, exhilarating and humbling, this is such a tale; an account of the awesome power of the sea and of the desperate human drama that unfolded in October 1991.

'Junger writes like a poet who has been to meteorology school'   RUTH RENDELL

The Diving-Bell and the Butterfly
Jean-Dominique Bauby

When a book is 'written' by a paralysed man flickering one eyelid, it might seem that the fact of writing is more remarkable than the book itself. Not when that book is *The Diving-Bell and the Butterfly*.

On December 9, 1995, Jean-Dominique Bauby suffered a massive stroke, locking his mind in the prison of his body. He then produced a work so unusual, moving and beautiful that it was published, read and admired around the world. With grace and economy, it describes his life before and after the stroke, his continuing imaginative freedom, and how he comes to terms with what has happened. It is a book that illuminates the very business of being alive.

'He goes to the core of what it means to be human'   *Observer*

Fermat's Last Theorem
Simon Singh

When a book about a fiendish mathematical conundrum tops the bestseller lists there is clearly something remarkable about it. Particularly when – unlike some scientific bestsellers – it is so enthusiastically read and recommended.

This brilliantly lucid account of three centuries of attempts to solve Pierre de Fermat's notorius mathematical theorem – and its eventual solution by an English mathematician who toiled in secret for years – opens the door on a hidden world of beauty and obsessive passion. It is a superb model of the readable but informative popular science book. And you *really* don't have to be a mathematician to enjoy it.

'Like the chronicle of an obsessive love affair. It has the classic ingredients that Hollywood would recognise'   *Daily Mail*

If You Liked This . . .
(continued)

The Lighthouse Stevensons
Bella Bathurst

This is the biography of an extraordinary family; a story of high endeavour and remarkable ingenuity, and of men pushed to the limit and beyond.

Robert Louis Stevenson may have been the most famous of the Stevensons but he was by no means the most productive. The Lighthouse Stevensons, all four generations of them, built every lighthouse around Scotland. Undaunted by formidable conditions, they achieved astonishing and innovative feats of engineering. The same formidable energy that Robert Louis put into his writing, his ancestors put into this visionary and inspiring quest to illuminate the seas.

'A splendid book which preserves the memory of great deeds performed in a heroic era'   *Sunday Times*

In the Heart of the Sea
Nathaniel Philbrick

One of the greatest sea yarns ever spun, *In the Heart of the Sea* is the true story of the extraordinary events which inspired Herman Melville's masterpiece *Moby-Dick*.

When the whaleship *Essex* set sail from Nantucket in 1819 the unthinkable happened. In the very furthest reaches of the South Pacific, she was rammed and sunk by an enraged sperm whale and her twenty crewmen forced to take to the open sea in three small boats. Ninety days later one surviving boat was rescued off the coast of South America – and a terrifying story of desperation, cannibalism and courage revealed.

'As gripping as it is grisly, with a cracking narrative and a terrible moral dilemma at its heart'   *Daily Mail*

*** * ***

Bad Blood
Lorna Sage

Hailed as one of most extraordinary memoirs of recent years, *Bad Blood* is a moving and devastatingly funny portrait of a family and a young girl's place in it.

Told with both passion and compassion, Lorna Sage here brings to life her girlhood in post-war provincial Britain. From the restrictions of the 40s to the freedoms of the 60s, this is an account of a life and times inextricably mixed. An international bestseller and prizewinner, *Bad Blood* is a brilliant exploration of family life and childhood memories – and of breaking the rules and breaking out.

'She lifts your spirits even as she hurts your heart'   ALLISON PEARSON

If You Liked This . . .
(continued)

Seabiscuit
Laura Hillenbrand

In 1938 one figure received more press coverage than Hitler, Mussolini and Roosevelt. He was a cultural icon and a world-class athlete – and an undersized, crooked-legged racehorse by the name of Seabiscuit.

Misunderstood and mishandled, Seabiscuit had spent seasons floundering in the lowest ranks of racing until a chance meeting of three men. Together, they created a champion. This is a story which topped the bestseller charts for over two years; a riveting tale of grit, grace, luck and an underdog's stubborn determination to win against all odds.

'A moving, emotion-charged rollercoaster'
Mail on Sunday

Toast
Nigel Slater

This is a coming of age with a difference – a culinary pilgrimage through the extraordinary childhood of award-winning food writer Nigel Slater. Moving and humorous in turn, it captures the tastes, treats and torments of daily life in 60s suburban England.

From Fray Bentos steak-and-kidney pie and cheese on toast to tapioca and Angel Delight, this is a remarkable, evocative portrait of childhood, adolescence and sexual awakening; a bitter-sweet bestseller served up with seasoning and flair.

'*Toast* connects emotions, memory and taste buds. Genius' LYNNE TRUSS

....

Reading Lolita in Tehran
Azar Nafisi
In Iran in the late 90s, Azar Nafisi and seven young women, her former students, met every Thursday to discuss forbidden works of Western literature. Shy and uncomfortable at first, they began to open up – not only about the novels they were reading but also about their own dreams and disappointments. Their personal stories intertwine with those they are reading – *Pride and Prejudice*, *The Great Gatsby* and *Lolita* – in this rare glimpse of women's lives in revolutionary Iran. A work of great passion and beauty, it is an uplifting account of quiet resistance in the face of repression.

'All readers should read it . . . engrossing, fascinating, stunning' MARGARET ATWOOD

....

The Motorcycle Diaries
Ernesto 'Che' Guevara
Che Guevara. Most of us know him now as a face on a T-shirt. These frank, irreverent diaries reveal the complex and appealing human being behind the iconic revolutionary image. ▶

If You Liked This . . .
(continued)

◄ In 1952, eight years before the Cuban revolution, two young men from Buenos Aires set out to explore South America on the back of a motorcycle. It was the journey of a lifetime, full of breathtaking scenery, hilarious escapades, and eye-opening encounters with poverty and exploitation. A journey on which Che discovered adventure, America and his own radical future.

'A revolutionary bestseller'   *Guardian*

Stuart
Alexander Masters
This is the story of Stuart Shorter: thief, hostage taker, psycho and street raconteur. It is also one of the most remarkable, moving and funny biographies ever written.

It is a story told backwards, as Stuart wanted, from the man he was when Alexander Masters met him, to a 'happy-go-lucky little boy' of twelve. Brilliant, humane and original, it is a prize-winning bestseller which is as extraordinary and unexpected as the life it describes.

'Bollocks brilliant. Possibly the best biography I have ever read' MARK HADDON ■